BRITAIN IN THE YEAR 2000

Britain in the Year 2000

Brian McConnell

NEW ENGLISH LIBRARY
TIMES MIRROR

An NEL Original
© 1970 by Brian McConnell

*

FIRST NEL EDITION OCTOBER 1970

*

NEL Books are published by
New English Library Limited from Barnard's Inn, Holborn, London E.C.1.
Made and printed in Great Britain by Hunt Barnard Printing Ltd., Aylesbury, Bucks.

45000687 5

Chapters

in the beginning . . .

> We shut our eyes to the beginnings of evil because
> they are small, and in this weakness lies the germ
> of our misfortune. *Principiis obsta:* this maxim
> closely followed would preserve us from almost
> all our misfortunes. . . . Amiel, *Journal Intime.*
> ii. 76.

IN THE beginning, according to the Good Book, there were the heavens and the earth. In thirty years' time, if the forecasters, pundits and other prophets of woe are to be believed, there will be little more than the heavens left.

The prospects for the earth as we know it today are grim.

Even allowing for error, there is peril in human behaviour – in the way we breed, in the food we eat, the air we breathe, the land we forage, the sea we fish. If truth is stranger than fiction, then the scientific truths now served us daily must seem to be the essence of phantasy. How else can we explain the watch on doom which is being maintained by professors, scientists, doctors and mass media? Mass hysteria? Hardly.

It is barely a year since the word 'ecology' was thrust at the reading, listening and television-viewing public. Yet ecology, only introduced as a word to the English language in the last century, has always been with mankind. It is the branch of biology which deals with all living things – and their modes of life – in relation to their surroundings. Others introduce the subject under the more easily understandable word: environment. Whatever the word, the subject compels earnest, immediate study.

Like many much publicised evils of the globe, the outcry about ecological and environmental study, or the lack of it, came from the North American landmass. There, the Friends of the Earth, Zero Population Growth, a plethora of preservation groups covering air and land traffic noise, pollution, natural conservation, birth control and wild life have all made their platforms and programmes known. City by city, Cleaner Air Weeks and similar campaigns from coast to coast have added practical demonstrations of the public awareness of the problems facing Americans today. So many organisations, campaigns and demonstrations have not unnaturally tended to give ecological and environmental studies a somewhat typical air of American exaggeration. And as each new threat to human life and all living organisms is announced, the people can be excused if they receive it like a very long running television serial, with more than a touch of unbelievable material running through it.

Yet no one can doubt that it is a very considerable problem, and one certainly not limited to the smog which settles over Los Angeles, the world's dirtiest city, or the red tide which poisons ocean life off the coast of Florida, or the massive oil-rig slick which fouled the beaches of Santa Barbara, California. The environmental problems the Americans scream about are world problems. Even the apparently clean lands are not unaffected. Scandinavia, with its façade of purity, suffers the massacre of fish in the effluent-ridden Norwegian fjords. The last time we saw Paris it was calculated that a person who stood still in a busy traffic sector would suffer, within three hours, a static pollution rising by 30 per cent. which could only be injurious to health, if not fatal. Cross over to Germany and find the Rhine, one of the world's largest sewers, emptying its filth into Holland, now acknowledged phlegmatically as the world's most unwilling cesspool.

The British have a natural counter instinct for believing, and acting as if, anything that happens in the United States of America could not happen here. Nor could the Plague, the Great Fire of London, or two World Wars. But they did. Natural and man-made doom is threatening Britain. The writing is not only on the wall but is written in the queues, traffic jams, overcrowded roads and cities, eroded coastlines, oily beaches, blighted countryside, dirty rivers and foul air. Out of all this has come the warning that a halt must be called to the population explosion, the manufacture of air polluting transport (not to mention its noise) the deposit of chemical and other wastes in the waters in and around the land, the poisoning of the countryside.

These evils did not just occur. They have been building up for years, decades, and in some instances centuries. It is only their altogether accumulation which has been realised suddenly by a growing public consciousness, by a better educated student body, stimulated by the age of protest in which its members live. The protests of students, their tutors, scientists and dons is – for once in the academic world of protest and demonstration – a considerable force for the good. For the time has been reached when something must be done about the crisis of the environment. The ignorance passed down the years means that the people cannot wait any longer for knowledge and for answers.

The purpose of this book is to give some of those answers, but first it will be necessary to trace the history of the crisis, and the antecedents of each of the particular branches of the threatening peril around us.

Broadly speaking, man by his sins of omission and commission, is responsible for it all. He has either harnessed the natural resources of the world, or failed to harness them correctly, so that these resources will now harm him. In his headlong rush to pioneer, invent, develop, he has forgotten or refused to employ the proper amount of checks and stops so that his creation for an immediate good is for ever in danger of threatening an ultimate evil.

He is not helped by the politicians and the planners, who are forever telling us that by the year 2000, in three short decades, our standards of living, like a crazy multiplication table, will have trebled. He is not told the cost. He is in danger of being lulled by the security consciousness of most politicians that within those thirty years poverty and homelessness will be

9

unknown, university education available to all, and the three day working week will be universally acceptable. In short, he is being led by politicians and planners into believing he can run into Utopia before being able to walk through his present existence.

Not surprisingly, any movement or campaign which threatens to halt this speedy passage of life towards the drawing-board Shangri-La is suspect, to be watched if not opposed. (We will be looking at how the suspect study of ecology is received by management and trade unions alike.) But meanwhile simple examples of the controversy are the most illustrative, and, at the same time, show the overall problem in its great complexity.

For instance, London is crying out for a third airport. It is necessary for comfort and convenience, but the moment Foulness, in the Thames Estuary, was mentioned as a possible site, the naturalists and ornithologists cried out: It will destroy the Brent geese which make their home there! Weary travellers, tired of the lack of proper airport-to-town facilities, screamed back: Who the hell cares about the Brent geese? They may be excused for not understanding the bird lovers' concern, or giving it second priority to the airport, but if we are to solve any part of the ecological crisis, there must be found a better all-round understanding of all living things, their comfort, their needs, and their natural heritage. And out of that understanding, the people will be able to seek a balance between their needs and what they can obtain without harm to others, or to too many others. Whether they can achieve that balance, without absolute government and punitive legislation, is a matter of further concern.

Consider an industrialist who, with his factory workers, know they must dump their chemical waste in a nearby river because, firstly there is nowhere else nearby to dispose of it, and, secondly, to take it elsewhere would prove so costly as to make their business or product uneconomic to pursue. A simple ban on dumping, or punitive fines, would rob the industrialist of his profits and the employees of their wages and both of their jobs. Surely here is an example of applying, and getting permission to use a factory site without anybody first considering the

10

order of good and harm that may come from such an enterprise. If, by chance, a local by-law covered such an act of pullution the enterprise was illegal to start with. If it was not so covered, as is usually the case, then the question arises whether, for the common good, some individual or authority should not seek redress under common law to stop pollution of the river. But then, in many cases, the feeling of local individuals and authorities might well be: If we want a clean river, and stop the factory from polluting it, who will be responsible for the employment of the people who will have no product to make and no waste to dump?

Consider also the issue of slum clearance in an overcrowded city. How easy to demand slum clearance, how difficult to achieve it, with full benefits. Slum dwellers are not unknown who prefer their homes, nearby friends, and social amenities that have been there as long as their unfit dwellings, to the new homes without friends and without social advantages. They often prefer to live in discomfort and with the risk of ill health but with the honesty, integrity, dignity and regularity of hard work close by than a move to a cleaner air zone but which involves them in travelling long distances to employment, often in or through an air polluted zone, using transport which further pollutes the atmosphere. Slum clearance without all the benefits is hardly slum clearance at all. Add to this the complexities of social life. Mix with it the racial problem of housing which besets West Indians in Brixton, London, Pakistanis in Bradford, Yorks, and even Roman Catholics and Protestants in Ulster. The environmental issues become more complex at every stage of the argument.

We will be looking at these issues in some more detail at a later stage in the book. For the moment, for the purpose of introduction, it is essential to see a glimpse of the dilemma. At the same time it is wise to think in terms of a list of apparently separate problems, the issues of potential evil, the demands for solution, the questions for realisation, and the balances of probability of success. The mind boggles at total, universal solution. Politicians and planners would turn from that suggestion in horror, neither having envisaged the task that has emerged from generations of planners and politicians who have lacked the foresight to see it in its enormity. We shall see what they have done. We shall see what can be done.

Pre-empting the issue of education, to be discussed later, it should be part of every child's earliest examination to be asked about the priorities as well as the facts of life. Which should come first? Housing the people, clothing the people, feeding the people or stopping the people who make the clothing from polluting the air and water which might make the otherwise well housed and well fed people very ill? Such questions would have a far more beneficial effect on the child and the child's eventual contribution to society than dealing with the eternal sequences of numbers, geometric symbols, and other alleged paraphernalia of intelligence quotients and educational ratios which disgrace most examination papers. Surely, since education is the principal means to a better way of life for the individual and society, their schooling should include as compulsory matters the scientific or artistic defence of human life and the living organisms on which that life depends.

More than that, the problems already touched on, and they are a fraction of the full crisis, are crying out for a whole system of educational curricula, of government and voluntary action, but above all a system of checks and stops at every level of child and adult development. It may be that eventually a supremo, a ministry of overall powers, a department of ecology and environment, rivalling even the Treasury in power, will be the only worthwhile solution. Meanwhile we can at least assert that if the educational issue is not tackled first, then the chances of eventually finding today's threats becoming tomorrow's realities will be far greater.

This urging of a greater awareness of the situation should not be taken or read to mean that Britain is totally unaware of the perils described. Her institutions, a free Press, the albeit more fettered and restricted television and radio media, Governmental and voluntary organisations, charities, and individuals motivated by more public good than private, are already some insurance against total apathy, lethargy, and even, sometimes, when all pleas look like coming to naught, against atrophy.

There has been, by any known monarchial standards, a remarkable lead given in these matters by Prince Philip, Duke of Edinburgh. Whatever the traditional restrictions on regal participation in controversial public matters, the presence of a consort with a public speaking manner which is forthright and encourages debate is a considerable advantage to open discussion on the issues of the day. Prince Philip accepted the Presidency of the World Wildlife Fund, an organisation devoted to preservation, and in this and other fields has led rather than prompted active public interest in retaining what is good in life. Prompting from the wings has its uses, but leading from the centre of the stage is by far the greater. Who else in the nation, which is short of a schooling system, central authority, or other guide to conservation, could arouse the public? When he states, as he did at Strasbourg, that to deal with the birth explosion we would have to put the pill in our daily bread, people sat up and took notice. Even the Americans, so much more obsessed with these matters, had their reservations removed when he said of Lake Erie: People who fall into that water don't drown. They just decay.

Prince Philip talks. People listen and then debate. What more must they do?

Troubles of the earth must be tackled at the roots, and despite the Princely and American examples already set – though in some cases because of them – there is required an overall catalogue of the problem and an overall solution. The youngsters of New Jersey, U.S.A., have dived into the Hackensack River and by hand removed the filth, rubbish and other foul agents which polluted it. All America, on Aprill 22, 1970, held an Earth Day. Philadelphia turned it into an Earth Week. One state college served rice to remind the partakers of world hunger. Other students have picketed motor car factories. In some towns (and Crawley, Sussex, England local council joined in) rubbish was dumped to prove how clean or dirty it was.

Out of all these examples one clear fact emerges. The roots of the human problem must be tackled first and foremost by the people. If as much energy was spent in preserving life as is spent in demonstrating against threatened death it would be a wholesome thing. The continual and endless marches to protest about bombs which might never be exploded could be put to more propaganda effect by demonstrating against agents which are already harming and destroying life which is assumed wrongfully to have a natural expectation of existence. If only all the energies expended (in copulation as well as marching, from Aldermaston to London) to protest about the existence of nuclear arms had been spent patrolling the oily beaches of our coasts . . . If, if, if.

Seldom has there been such a weapon in the hands of the people, who, sooner or later, must vote and elect people on the one solitary issue of who will do most to ensure that they live a purer, cleaner, fuller and more healthy life than they do today. For whom should we vote? For the politician who promises technological advances or for he who promises conservation? For those who would have difficulty in making up their minds, ponder this thought. The very people who escaped the massacres and charnel houses of World War II are the same people who today are threatened by biological and chemical changes, often called advancements and improvements, which can eventually kill them. Even if the preference is for a later death than sooner, there is an alternative of a better life which will last longer and culminate in death very much later by more natural means.

If only we could plan conservation and preservation as we plan these alleged advances. But then planning, within its own short disorderly life, has brought the very word into disrepute. If anyone requires proof of the foolhardiness of planners just look at the railways which criss-cross the land. When the iron road came to these shores the rolling stock barons laid their lines where they would. The people and their industries, if perchance they were not already there, had to move to the railway lines. If they were in the wrong place, then the railways were laid as masters of their lives, to their discomfort. Just look today from the railway carirage windows as your train trundles by, only a few feet from the living room windows of some unfortunate's home. Much of which has existed for more than 100 years.

Not even the great social revolution of 1945, which followed World War II, solved such problems. Despite the setting up of local planning committees of recommendation, county planning authorities with powers of decision, courts of inquiry and tribunals of appeal, and even ministers to sit in judgement, there is still no planning system of material and structural needs worthy of this country. What hope can there be, then, for a planning system which covers the more essential salvation of life already in existence, the nurturing of life to come?

It may be that the absence of the will to plan at national (before considering international) level will put paid to that question. It may be that the various demands on Britain, public as well as private, cannot be equated to the extent of planning and providing the best for most, if not all, people. Can anyone explain how in the great county of London in the year 1970 a motorway is built with an elevation which passes within eleven feet of a human being's bedroom window; traffic is allowed to pass by on the carriageway emitting a noise measured at nine times the level calculated to be injurious to health; and how then, and only then, does authority consider that the miserable dwellers should be rehoused? If that takes place under the name of planning, a new philosophy must emerge, a new concept develop of how to resolve the enigmas of, first, the more simple elements of living, before the conundrums of the machine age, automobiles, their pollution and noise are reached. After that, perhaps, the even more up-to-date threats of radiation, nerve gas, and other evils may be tackled. Even in 1970, there must be a start at the beginning, a progression, and still then there is a very long way to go.

It is certain that man, by misuse and by neglect, has already damaged much of his environment beyond repair. Now we must look to see what is irreparable, and move quickly to prevent a repetition of destruction. Our adult population might well wish to deny their responsibility, but they should be warned. There is a growing generation now aware of this crisis, a generation which will not wait for the answers. Already, even before the ink on these pages is dry, they have ceased to marvel at their parents' reckless, hell bent expansion and development

15

to the detriment of living organisms. They are interested in interplanetary exploration, but they are more concerned that earth does not become as lifeless as the Moon, that the atmosphere of this planet does not become as inhospitable as that of others.

If we can calculate what is irreparable we must readily accept that in many respects this is the last opportunity we will have to right the wrongs of decades. How all the evils are put right is a matter of discussion and action by individuals, then in groups, by discussions, by teach-ins, by classes, by lectures, by conferences. Those who claim they have no time for such group co-operation might do worse than writing some observation about the decay, destruction and pollution about them to the Editor of their local newspaper or to their Member of Parliament. Whatever they do, and as soon as they do it, they wil be drawing the attention of at least one more person to the environmental crisis which faces us. Eventually there will be large scale, concerted and effective national action.

To this end this book is devoted.

To achieve this end we require a number of answers. We require a very much larger understanding of ecology in all its forms. Then must come the knowledge of what can and should be preserved. From then we can take up scientific and technological know-how which will help us to control pollution in all its forms, to conserve what is best, and to build on the life we have preserved. All this next will demand a series of priorities of which is the most important, not merely which is possible, probable, impossible or improbable. And when we are equipped with all that we must find a governmental system under which laws are framed, and are properly administered.

How soon can this be done? That is in the laps of the people. To help them understand this volume has been prepared to show a picture of life thirty years hence, in A.D. 2000, at the turn of the century. By the time those three decades have elapsed, the people will have decided by how much or by how little they can control their own environment. So far they have indicated a lip service, following the shock propaganda of 1970, a year of publicity on the subject. European Conservation Year,

16

1970, the promise of a five year assault on the European problems of environment, followed by the 1972 Stockholm United Nations Conference of Environment promises well for propaganda.

But how soon will the public tackle the problem of piecemeal laws and machinery which has been developing for more than a century to control pollution? How quickly will they realise that ill health by itself is not the all important threat, but that assaults on the pleasure, contentment and quality of life must be combated first to prevent an ill-health which, at present, no one has yet fully experienced? How much longer will it take for these problems to be tackled and then solved?

On paper the picture of Britain in the year 2000 is not an attractive one. Only those who take up these issues now will be able to change that picture.

the birth explosion

(It was the custom among Jews and other ancient races to place a newly born child upon the ground immediately after its birth.)

The infant, as soon as Nature with great pangs of travail hath sent it forth from the womb of its mother into the regions of light, lies, like a sailor cast out from the waves, naked upon the earth, in utter want and helplessness, and fills every place around with mournful wailings and piteous lamentations, as is natural for one who has so many ills of life in store for him, so many evils which he must pass through and suffer.

. . . Bacon, *De Rerum Natura.* v. 223.

THE WHOLE problem of the ecological or environmental crisis is a matter of birth and death. It is pointless discussing food shortages, lungs diseased by foul air, deafness brought about by incessant noise, without talking about the root of the matter, the birth and death issue.

Statistics tend to bore, but these figures show that this nation of ours has borne the following populations:

1801	11,944,000 total, with	5,692,000 males,	6,252,000 females
1851	22,259,000	10,855,000	11,404,000
1901	38,237,000	18,492,000	19,745,000
1951	50,225,000	24,118,000	26,107,000
1966	53,788,000	26,048,000	27,745,000

Now the Government actuary, in consultation with the Registrar General, has noted this rise in the birth rate:

1938	735,573 births or 15.15 per thousand of the population
1961	944,000	17.8
1968	949,200	17.2

At the same time the death rate has gone like this:

1938	559,598 deaths or 12.6 males, 11.0 females per thousand
1961	631,788	12.6	11.4
1968	656,000	11.9 per thousand.

From those figures, the demographers calculate that the estimated future population of the United Kingdom will be:

1970	55,989,000
1971	56,295,000
1972	56,617,000
1975	57,653,000
1980	59,548,000
1999	64,216,000
2000	70,339,000

If the figures have that stark mystical unreality to the reader, as such tables often have, then they might be compared without detail to the population situation in other countries. For all China's teeming millions and India's vast populace, Britain's population density is three times that of China's and one and a half time's as much as India's. When one considers the United States' concern about environment, one should remember that its citizen's live at a density of only fifty-seven people to the square mile compared with 588 people per square mile in the United Kingdom. Restricted to England the problem is far worse with 911 people per square mile, and one might be forgiven for thinking that on a mathematical basis a density problem sixteen times as great as that in the U.S.A. must mean sixteen times the environmental problem, too.

The author has taken the conservative official estimates rather than those generally used in ecological discussion. Lord Kennett, a former parliamentary secretary to the Ministry of

Housing and Local Government addressing a women's conference at Scarborough, Yorkshire, in March, 1970, estimated Britain's total population in the year 2000 as well over 100,000,000.

Whichever figure is chosen, the official 70,339,000 or the ministerial 100,000,000 estimate, the question to ponder is what would life be like for those people. The living density would increase. More homes, schools, university places, and more employment would have to be found. Since density is already a problem, since there are already homeless and people living in substandard housing conditions, since the schools and hospital building programmes are the subject of constant criticism, and since there is still an unemployment problem, the prospect cannot be regarded as short of frightening.

Population is the principal determinant of the whole crisis. To increase the population is but human. Humanity decides that cohabitation, just as the churches lay down that through marriage, is for the procreation of children. Human frailty, with or without marriage, decides whether too many or too few children are born into the world. They are facts which cannot be denied by politician or preacher, and which cannot be altered by law or lecture, except by the most gross interference with freedom.

Science, though now in its most ultra commercial form, has given cohabiting couples a series of controls to prevent too many unnecessary, unwanted, or unneeded children coming into the world. While the churches preached restraint or no restraint, the scientific-commercial world introduced the more practical and humanly compulsive devices of the condom, inter uterinery fitments, and, if all that failed, abortion as the only answer. It may be, to use the politicians' most popular excuse, that you cannot legislate against morality or the lack of it, but the first condemnation of mankind in Britain today is that in dealing with childbirth, either on moral or practical grounds, the nation cannot even get its priorities right.

To begin with, there is a traditional failure and objection to dealing with sex education in a necessary and logical manner.

Broadly speaking there are those who believe that sex education is the prerogative of the parents and those who believe it
is the duty of the schoolteachers. There may be nothing that a
parent would not do for a child, and there may be nothing that
a schoolteacher would not do for a pupil, but the unhappy fact
is that in the vast majority of cases, in the field of sex education,
the parent and schoolteacher do nothing for the child. The play-
ground, the quadrangle, the lavatory walls, and the first teenage
romp between male and female on an untended, unwatched bed
are still the best known classrooms for sex education.

With such a beginning to life, while the parent and schoolteacher continue to argue the best way to teach children, it is
not surprising that the competition between birth, birth control
and abortion still have priority over a commonsense approach
to the subject. As long as those battles continue the population
will continue to be unrestricted, And, although we have here
used actuarial tables to indicate the growth tendency, demography is still an uncertain science subject to those human
frailties and uneducated humans.

So it will continue until those battles are resolved. They are
not to be oversimplified.

Supposing it was universally agreed that a proper, acknowledged and universal system of sex education was evolved and
put into practice, it would still be subject to human error and
temptation. When a man and/or a woman experiences temptation, then how can they stop a child being born? The psychia-
trists now enter the conflict. The use of coitus interruptus,
the withdrawal of the male organ before ejaculation, has been
alternately described as a serious non-event to a serious de-
pressant for the parties involved. The condom has been con-
demned because it is a repressant and fails to give human satisfaction. Other reasons have been advanced for a woman not
using an inter-uterinery device. So, after a child is conceived,
abortion may be ordered.

It is ludicrous that the State, with its massive National Health
Service, education-for-all organisation, cannot in the first
instance provide birth control advice and help for even a substantial proportion of the population. How else can one describe

21

a nation in which comparatively few local authorities will make grants to voluntary family planning organisations and clinics at the ratepayer's expense, while those same ratepayers (and, as taxpayers) must contribute to a National Health Service, the duty of which is to prevent suffering as well as cure it. Successive governments have preferred that the same conscience which leaves sex education willy nilly to the individual must also leave the provision of family planning and abortion to similar uncertain individuals and organisations.

What contribution is being made to halt the birth bomb, which, if not checked, will be far more devastating in the discomfort, torture, and other eventualities than anything devised for warfare?

Once there was a move to deter Cockneys from making their late summer exodus to the hop fields of Kent because the close, cramped and often primitive conditions in which they lodged were accepted by medical officers of health as an assured forecast of a higher birth rate nine months later. In Baden-Wurtemberg, Germany, the 1970 World Cup for soccer enthusiasts was welcomed because so many men watched the series on international television that it left them too tired for love making or procreating children. Alas, the prospects of scientific population control are remote.

Even Lord Kennett, the former minister, put forward situations rather than solutions. Only three things could halt the world population explosion, he said, and they are war, starvation or contraception. Nor could he offer any urgent solution. 'Although it is not yet time for a government policy about the problem, research and public discussion should go ahead', he said. 'People should decide what level of population could be tolerated and how the level could be maintained.'

This may be a fallacy. Prince Philip told a European Conservation conference in Strasbourg that something must be done to muffle the population explosion – already at plague proportions.

'Somebody is going to have to devise a policy to put the pill in bread or something.'

The Prince, vice-Chairman of the Board of Sponsors of the

conference said the population explosion threatened to undermine the social structure. 'The increase in population has created cities bigger than the world has ever seen and intense overcrowding in almost all parts of the country', he said.

Now demography is an inexact science, and the estimated project figures already quoted, and the consequences that might arise from them stated, may be wanting in proof. Yet short of very unscientific miracles, nothing put forward at the time of writing can possibly reverse the trend. To illustrate the confusion facing demographers, let us compare two important surveys on what mothers, married or not, are supposed to want.

According to Dr Ann Cartwright, research director of the medical research unit, Bethnal Green, almost half of Britain's mothers have had a baby they did not want or did not expect. And more than a quarter of babies born are the result of pregnancies which occurred when couples were practising birth control. From that survey of births and birth control carried out in twelve districts of England and Wales, Dr Cartwright discovered that a doctor's response to family planning inquiries seemed to depend far too much on his or her age, sex or religion. Doctors actually questioned admitted that they rarely raised the subject of family planning during conversation with patients.

Only 20 per cent. said that they would introduce the topic to a married woman with three children with no social and health problems. Only 23 per cent. would introduce the subject with a woman patient getting married.

Miss Jean Thompson, a government statistician, after a survey among 7,000 women of various backgrounds and social circumstances, told an all party House of Commons committee that they would like larger families, three or four children each, if they could afford them, but to maintain their present standard of living they restricted the size of their families and the average number is kept to two or three. These women are largely the girls born to the wives of returning World War II servicemen who were having children of their own, so that one birth explosion was being replaced by another. Their children, in turn, if not restricted, will repeat the process.

That is why, in the evidence to the committee, it was revealed

23

that by the year 2000 the number of children under 14 will jump by one third. The under 14 population of 1970 is 13,200,000. By the end of the century this figure will be 17,600,000. The problem this teenage bulge will bring will be more clearly indicated in a moment.

Sir Solly Zuckerman, the Government's chief economic adviser, in a report to the former Prime Minister, Mr Wilson, indicated that every aspect of life would be under pressure. Unless immediate steps are taken, he said, it will become even more difficult to find jobs, homes, hospital beds and school places. As a result of Sir Solly's warning, the Government set up a team to study 'what the birthrate figures may mean for the quality of life in the future'.

In his report, Sir Solly capsuled the problems. 'In the remaining thirty years of this century, provisions may have to be made for almost as many additional people as has been accommodated in the first seventy years.' If that sounds terrifying, there is certainly food for thought in Sir Solly's own belief that Britain could support more than twice its present population if we were prepared to live like battery hens, something which could be done, he believes, without the system breaking down.

Is there no limit to the population that this country could contain? 'If one assumes that human beings have not got ideas of their own on how they want to live, we could house people in batteries, assuming that the technology and trade were right. I could see this island containing not seventy million or maybe less, in the year 2000, but 240 million. I think its conceivable.'

One must be forgiven for throwing doubt on the views of so eminent a scientist, for it is seldom that human behaviour, or the technological and trade trends, can be equated with scientific prophecy no matter how honest that prophecy, or with what skill it has been arrived at. Despite the forecasts of population, Sir Solly advises that while the increasing population trend is 'serious' he avers, 'I do not believe we have reached the optimum point at this stage. I cannot see any revolutionary stop which could be taken by the Government now. His Population Study Group would, however, continue to keep a close eye on the situation to try to identify the approach of danger level so that the Government could, when necessary, take action, although neither he nor any other Government adviser, official or spokesman has been able to indicate what action that might be.

Not surprisingly, with the weight of this advice, Mr James Callaghan, former Home Secretary; Mr Anthony Crosland, former Secretary for Local Government and Regional Planning; and Lord Kennet, former Parliamentary Secretary, Ministry of Housing, took precisely the same view. It is difficult to see, in the overall picture, how Mr Crosland particularly could subscribe to that opinion in place of urgency. For the population trends show that in the increase of numbers in the next three decades there is evidence of considerable regional problems. If the population rises to 68,000,000 (the least figure suggested) or 70,000,000 (the upper rounded figure) there is more than a likelihood that the most densely populated areas will be the south east of England with 27,000,000 people, and the north-west, with more than 8,000,000.

The south east area includes Bedfordshire, Berkshire, Buckinghamshire, Essex, Hampshire, Hertfordshire, Surrey, East and West Sussex, the Isle of Wight, and Poole, Dorset. Perhaps the populations of these districts if they examined the prospects might feel a greater sense of urgency than do their masters and servants in Whitehall. If they do not there is a growing army of people who do.

One expert suggests shock steps to curb the population explosion which, he says, is threatening the quality of life in Britain.

Dr Aubrey Manning of Edinburgh University recommends a financial reward for public submitting to sterilisation. And a system of annual tax-free bonuses for women of child bearing age who do not produce a child during the year.

To preserve our present living standards without cutting the birth rate we would have to build a new city the size of Leeds every year, he says in a new magazine *The Ecologist*. 'If we could eliminate every unwanted birth in Britain, we could probably stop our population growth almost at once.'

But, he adds, most Christian leaders seem more worried by

25

the supposed threat to conventional sexual morality posed by contraception than by the benefits it can mean in the reduction of births. Of course, when restraint fails Britain should launch an immediate crash programme to reduce the birth rate – including incentives to women to stay childless. 'We have been disastrously slow to recognise how population pressure constitutes a threat to our future. The effects of population growth are slow and insidious.'

Dr Manning said that contrary to the predictions of the politicians, Britain is facing a situation in which the quality of life is sure to decline. 'It is quite wrong to assume that our small islands can go on for ever keeping us not just in the manner to which we are accustomed, but with an ever-rising standard of living. Britain already suffers from the pollution of affluence. Everyone expects a vast range of material things including a heated house, access to lucrative work, a hospital service, thirty gallons of clean water every day and the use of a car. These requirements make each Briton equivalent in consumer terms to at least twenty Indians living in their own country on the bare essentials of subsistence. But already we in Britain average 226 people for each square kilometer of land – one and a half times more than India and ten times more than the U.S.A. At present our population is about 55 million and although our birth rate is currently falling there is still a daily surplus of births over deaths of more than 800.

'Every day eight hundred extra Britons join us with their rights and expectations of the good life. If we are to meet those it means the equivalent of four hundred new houses and a new school every day, a new hospital every month or a new city the size of Leeds every year. There are no signs that these requirements can be met. At the present moment we have an enormous backlog of house, school and hospital building and clearly we cannot hope to catch up so long as our population continues to increase.

'No matter how well we try to plan development there can be no end to waiting lists for houses, overcrowded classrooms, congested roads and all the other drawbacks of continual growth.'

26

The bewildered layman can be excused if he cannot choose between the studied patience and cool of Sir Solly and the impatient enthusiasm in ecology of Dr Manning. He may find enlightenment in the precept of ignoring the crystal ball of the year 2000 while the facts of 1970 are available. These facts show that none of the public and social services available to today's population are adequate or efficient by any minimal standards, and that begets the question of how can they reach such a lowly standard in thirty years to serve a greatly increased population.

*   *   *

The question of population explosion dealt with here has not taken into account the ever present problem of immigration. That is a subject made unseasonable by racialists and politicians who are committed to viewpoints which cannot be altered by facts or figures. It is not the purpose of this work to support or deny their claims.

The facts are as follows: Some 250,000 people emigrate from our shores each year, and if the environmental crisis grows in severity then it is reasonable to suppose that this figure will increase. At the same time, there is the hidden figure – and the statistics are not known – of those who, disillusioned by life abroad, return. They may return for a variety of reasons and the discomforts described in these chapters may well be among them.

Immigration, despite legal restrictions, is increasing.

The Institute of Race Relations, which could hardly be described as inflaming race relations, was more frank than Government departments in its famous report 'Colour and Citizenship'. They said that in 1966 there were 924,000 coloured people in England and Wales – 710,900 born overseas, 213,300 born here. By 1986, this figure is likely to rise to between 2,074,000 and 2,373,000 – or between four and five of every 100 of the population.

Who are these people whose numbers will more than double in twenty years?

Of the 317,900 adult West Indians born overseas, the early

immigrants were more skilled than those who arrived later, and they came in response to labour demands.

Of the 290,000 Indians and Pakistanis most came because of the partition of their two countries, when they had to leave and seek new homes and jobs.

The vast majority of coloured immigrants – more than seventy out of every 100 – live in big cities and suburbs and almost half of them in London.

Despite their growth, though, they do not represent more than one or two per cent. of the populations in the districts where they live. Men outnumbered women by a very large ratio when immigration began, but this is levelling out among West Indians – thirteen men to every ten women. Indian and Pakistani men, though number forty-two to every ten women.

Although immigrant women used to have children more often that women born in Britain, this rate is falling.

Immigrant homes are more crowded than those of the English. At the same time, coloured people own their own homes in twice as many cases as English people do – in proportion to their numbers.

In Birmingham, forty-eight out of every 100 coloured homes are owner-occupied. In London, it's fifty-six out of every 100.

Some of the future can be gauged from these capsuled facts and it would be folly to pretend that they do not add to the solution of the population problem. The bitter population pill is not more easily swallowed by palatable reports that the fertility level will fall. The report summarises the fertility situation as follows:

'Migrants are generally young, under thirty years of age when they move, and generally single. After settling into the new community, new alliances, usually within the supportive atmosphere of each ethnic minority, lead to marriage and the procreation of new offspring. The initial imbalance between males and females in the immigrant population is redressed by marriage outside the group or by the later arrival of eligible mates. The delay in marriage which is consequent upon migration and the time it takes to settle into the new community usually lowers overall fertility compared with the ring in the home country or at least delays it.'

Just as demography as a science is inexact, so social t.. as described in the report, cannot be accepted as an accurate guide to the future. We have noted that Britons are not educated in, nor encouraged to use, family planning. This is even more true of immigrants. Whether immigrants marry among themselves or intermarry with residents, the logical and arithmetical result is that more babies will be born. On that note we leave the population explosion, and consider what the unwanted or surplus people of Britain can look forward to in the years up to 2000.

Whatever their origin, whatever their race, colour or creed, the people will face the same problems of social services unable to keep pace with demand. As long ago as October, 1967, the Government stated that it was proposed, in the ensuing ten years, to spend some £1,000,000,000 on new hospital buildings. But after three of those ten years the impact of new buildings on the shortage of hospital beds appears negligible.

This problem is apparent from the womb to the tomb. Even before a new birth, or to prevent a new birth, the availability of hospital beds is a prime example of a state being unable to support its people. It is scandalous. For the nation, having got its priorities so wrong, has put the termination of life as more important than the preservation of existing life. A woman needing a gyneacological operation, for the sake of her own health, if not for a child she wants, must wait for a National Health Service bed up to a year because that bed is needed for abortion cases.

Dr Joseph Dignan, an experienced general medical practitioner of East London, and chairman of the North East Metropolitan Executive Council of the National Health Service, has charged that some doctors shop around for beds for their patients. Even doctors who accept fees from private patients, and cannot find beds in which their abortions can be carried out, use their influence to obtain beds in National Health Service hospitals, which should go to poorer patients with probably more urgent need. As a result a wealthy woman from

Birmingham can get a bed in a London hospital, while a local woman of less means must wait up to twelve months for her operation. And this problem is not confined merely to London and Birmingham.

Most hospitals are so embarrassed by the situation that they decline to give figures, and the Department of Health can only say, somewhat lamely, that the waiting list for gynaecological operations has fallen nationally from 83,297 at December 31, 1967 to 82,787 a year later. Having failed to decide on a family planning scheme for the nation, the state must pay so much attention to abortions that other operations must wait, and wait to an extent that makes nonsense of socialised medicine, and a mockery of medical ethics.

But the scandal of the hospital bed shortage does not end there, as we will see by looking at the plight of young children. In Birmingham, fifty children have suffered permanent damage to their hearing because they had to wait for hospital treatment. An inquiry has been set up to examine the problem, but it will not repair the damage to the children. Even in the non emergency categories the delays are appalling. Twelve months for non emergency operations is usual, while patients awaiting surgery for hernia, varicose veins and similar painful conditions are waiting much longer. The reasons are not so easy to ascertain.

Principally, the shortage of beds and staff are offered as the reasons, but ineffective use of many hospital units and a greater willingness among the public to undergo hospital treatment has been more than a contributory factor. Education and public opinion – particularly in gynaecological operations – have changed greatly in the past twenty years. As a result the number of hospital in-patients has risen by a total of 70 per cent. since the N.H.S. began in 1948, while the numbers of doctors and nurses has increased, by comparison, only fractionally.

Add to this the problem of under-use of hospital units and the problem appears in greater perspective. Many older hospitals are very much out of date and are not being replaced, or modernised fast enough. Some are known to be underoccupied by 50 per cent. The hospitals are in places which do not attract doctors, where consultants can only visit at sparse and infrequent intervals, and surgeons may be only able to perform operations at a maximum of once a week. The patients they visit can, therefore, be only admitted on infrequent occasions and intervals which explains why – in a Welsh survey – an ear, nose and throat patient would stay 5.6 days in a hospital bed, when that bed would then remain empty for 4.9 days before the next patient could be brought in.

All this is despite a fall in a limited number of complaints which demanded hospitalisation, such as polio, tonsillectomy, adenoidal operations, ulcers, tuberculosis, but because of a steep rise in other more modern and common ailments. None of these is more serious than the demand for beds by mental patients, and they require special, separate hospital units to care for them.

Dr G. Wyn Griffith, contributing to *Health Trends*, calculated that without psychiatric patients, hospital admissions had increased by nearly one third between 1957 and 1967. The 1958 admissions totalled 3,554,700 while the 1967 figure was 4,605,050. And there were barely enough beds to accommodate such large numbers. At the same time, the state, unable to expand hospital units to cater for more in-patients, curiously underestimated the needs of mental patients, as indicated in a damning indictment by Dr F. M. Martin and Mr G. F. Rehin, in a study, *Towards Community Care*. These mental health specialists recalled that the Hospital Plan of 1962 foreshadowed a need for only 92,000 hospital beds in 1975, which was already a fall of 60,000 from the 1960 estimate. Yet there were, in fact, still nearly 140,000 beds available in 1967.

Here we have a situation in which the former Ministry of Health, obviously unaware of the strains and stresses modern society is placing upon the mental health of the country, planning to reduce by massive proportions the availability of beds for the victims. Even allowing for the arguments that not all mental patients in mental hospitals should be there, and should be in some other kind of rehabilitative unit, there is a dismal prospect for those unfortunates who suddenly suffer mental disorder and find they cannot be accommodated. Particularly

31

when one remembers that these unfortunates are the largest single group of the seriously ill.

The 1968 National Association for Mental Health Report said that well over 500,000 people were receiving care or treatment for mental disorders and 47 per cent. of hospital beds available were occupied by the mentally ill. Between 1956 and 1967, the number of patients in hospitals for the mentally ill fell from 150,000 to 121,000, but the number of patients admitted for the first time nearly doubled. The total number of admissions rose from 83,994 to 169,160, and new patients rose from 127,000 to 191,000. While the average stay in hospitals for the mentally ill fell from 100 days in 1956 to 69 days in 1966, seven out of every ten patients had been in hospital for two years or more. Lord Balniel, chairman of that association, summed up the situation with the words, 'Such people as the mentally disordered are often inarticulate or confused, and society has a special duty to bring them comfort and help to alleviate their distress. . . . There are something like twice as many mentally disabled people being treated in the community as in mental hospitals. . . . And it is estimated that one third of the patients seen by family doctors are suffering from illness that is mental or emotional in origin.'

What hope for these unfortunates if the state cannot make provision, within a reasonable degree of accuracy, for their future? What a commentary on a society that produces them and then cannot care for them!

It may be that taking hospitalisation as a whole too much attention is paid to keeping patients in bed in hospital. Dr Robert Logan, director of the Medical Care Research Unit at Manchester University, has advanced the view that medicine, having cleared the more common infectious diseases, is left with a hard core of chronic degenerative illnesses, which will increase as we keep people alive to suffer them. The remedy, in his view, is to reduce the length of hospital stay. Bring the national average stay down to nine days – the average reported in Sheffield and Oxford – and the national average waiting list will be cleared within little more than a year.

Hernia cases in England and Wales are kept in hospital on

an average for fourteen days while in Sweden and the United States they leave hospital after nine days.

While reducing hospital stay to mathematical proportions, it is as well to remember that human nature tends to demand more attention from doctors than doctors should give it. There is a psychology among patients which demands, nay boasts about, the time they should remain in hospital. Yet there is powerful support for sending them out much earlier than hitherto. Sir George Godber, for Chief Medical Office, Department of Health, is concerned about the length of stay, particularly by the 117,000 hernia and 49,000 varicose veins in-patients each year.

He believes that there should be more one day beds because perhaps one third of all in-patients in acute wards could be dealt with without being kept in for more than twenty-four hours. And experience, he says, has shown that many could be treated, not as in-patients at all, but on an out-patient basis.

He may well be right, but if this type of argument has only reached this stage in 1970, what will be the situation three decades hence? If the population continues to grow, as envisaged, the problem of how to treat patients, whom to hospitalise, and how many beds they will need, should have already been solved and the answer put into effect. For if we do not solve quickly the problem of today's common ailments and illnesses, we will be unlikely to be in time to deal with those which come later.

In such a disarray of problems about health, or the lack of it, the prevention, the treatment and the cure, who can deny that the increased population now envisaged would be indeed a deprived population? A nation with a disorderly health system could not fail to be an unhealthy nation.

Every generation has its social problems, and these may be patched and repaired though never solved. But when the next generation is so swollen in number that no amount of repair and patching can sustain the social system then ecological disaster has arrived.

If a child does survive the hospital system, he or she can look forward to other hazards in the education system. Who has not heard of slum schools, overcrowded classes? The shortage of

33

teachers, the lack of teaching space seems forever with us. If we cannot overcome such shortages and shortcomings for the children with us now, and the children who will soon need education, it is most unlikely that the problem will lessen in three decades when so many youngsters seek schooling. Add to this the prospect of raising the school leaving age in 1972, without any demand or prospect of raising the school entry age, and yet another field of ecology reaches dangerous proportions.

At one end of the scale, in this acquisitive society, more employers are offering more married women work, without either the State or industry offering her sufficiently more nurseries or nursery schools to care for her children while she toils. At the other end of the ladder, the clamour for more higher education for more adolescents also grows.

There is grave concern that the universities will not be able to accommodate the rapidly increasing student population. Lord Bowden, Principal of Manchester University Institute of Science and Technology, has told the court of governors that university sizes will have to be trebled in a decade in order to accommodate the estimated 450,000 students – double the present number – that will be seeking varsity education in 1980. Lord Shawcross, Chancellor of Sussex University, has warned his court of governors of government cuts in university spending which will, in the long term interests of Britain, be disastrous. And these warnings come at a time when the increase in admissions is a mean 3 per cent. per year.

Who now can say the population explosion is not a matter of urgent attention? In the next thirty years the increase in population, plus the inadequacies of the health service, plus the deficiencies of the schools, plus the automation of industry which will rob many of their jobs, plus the increasing burden of the elderly on the population, will altogether present a dilemma, which, if not tackled now, will bring the nation to a state of chaos which will not be capable of harmonising by normal, natural orderly means.

the empty plate

> Let us never forget that the cultivation of the earth is the most important labour of man.
> . . . Daniel Webster, *Speech: The Agriculture of England*, Boston, 1840.

EVEN IF the population of Britain and of the world can be kept down to manageable proportions, there will be ever present the question of how to feed the people. As long ago as 1946 an international body was set up to deal with this problem.

Sir John Boyd Orr, Director-General of the United Nations Food and Agriculture Oraginsation, called an urgent conference of that organisation to establish a permanent world food board to replace the present temporary world food council.

It was proposed that the board should stabilise prices in international markets, build up a world reserve of food and develop agriculture in backward countries. Food, agriculture, and international trade and finance organisations, would be represented on this board. 'If we do not have this, or some plan of this kind', he said, 'you will have a most awful agricultural crisis in 1949, or even 1948 if there are bumper harvests in 1947.'

In 1949 Europe would reach a pre-war level of food production, and unless nations were ready to cope with surpluses thrown on the market there would be no purchasing power for them and prices would crash. The crisis would come much more quickly than ever before. Already the food balance sheet was greatly improved and harvests in all countries were more than promising.

The Board would have funds to build up a world reserve of food. When products fell below a certain price the board would take them into reserve and when world prices tended to rise above a certain level it would release the reserves to stabilise prices.

He believed the plan would result in the gradual elimination of hunger, a greatly expanding market for agriculture accompanied by guaranteed prices and a tremendous demand for industrial products. There would be an enormous increase in international standards of life. Something had to be done quickly because the Emergency World Food Council would finish in 1947. If the feeding of the world was to be brought up to a healthy standard world production of food had to be increased by about 100 per cent. Even the production of cheap cereals neded to be increased because hundreds of millions of people were hungry at a time when wheat was being burnt.

At the first meeting of the Utopian sounding World Food Council, Sir John called for 'bold and far-reaching action' in tackling current food shortages and future 'unmarketable surpluses'. If the nation's efforts were turned to agriculture as they had been to war, a world of hunger could be turned into a world of plenty in five years, he said. But even then the food situation was deteriorating, and the gap between the demand and supply of grain was growing. The famine which had stalked Bengal in 1943 was still being repeated in India and other lands, and wartime rationing in Britain had to be continued long after the war ended.

Starving India and rationed Britain survived those late 1940s crises, but even then Sir John warned: 'Further economic shocks on an already distracted and impoverished world may lead to a complete breakdown in the structure of human society.'

Sir John, later Lord Boyd Orr, was right, but the full reasons could not have then been apparent. His policy, translated by the F.A.O., was that 'if immediate and long range plans to free the world from hunger are carried through by the United Nations, of which both the supplying and receiving countries are members, the provision of food can be put on a business

36

footing. In this way there need be no humiliating pauperism on the part of receiving nations. If such an action is not taken there is a danger that the world economic and political situation will become worse'.

The natural tendency was to look not just first but only at the underdeveloped countries. In doing so, the F.A.O. most probably underestimated the needs of Europe. In looking at the problem as it would develop, and might be solved, by the year 2000, the Organisation calculated that the potential capacity for increasing food production throughout the world was very substantial indeed, though the regions where more food and better diets were most urgently needed were precisely those where the problem of keeping pace with an expanding population was considered to be most critical. That is to say that the problem was, to the F.A.O., a non-European problem.

An F.A.O. study dealt with the physical potentialities of raising production to meet the requirements expected to be present at the end of the century, on the basis that the world population would double between 1963 and that date. To feed these people, this international body estimated that there would be required a fourfold increase in Asia and the Far East, a threefold or fourfold rise in Latin America, a threefold increase in the Near East, and a step up of between two and three times in Africa.

This would be necessary to ensure, by AD 2000, a diet of about 2,400 calories a day, including 20 grammes of animal proteins, in the underdeveloped regions. All very laudable, but the plan was dependent upon too many contingencies. In Latin America and Africa, the physical resources were unquestionably ample, but, said the study, 'the outcome would depend primarily on the establishment of progressive and stable governments that are willing and able to mobilise their own resources and make effective use of foreign aid'. While this hope has not been fulfilled, the Organisation warned, 'The rate of destruction of resources in some parts of Africa is causing considerable concern.'

The Near East problem was that, quite apart from the political considerations, such an increase in food production would be difficult without greater technical progress, and probably impossible without massive irrigation and a solution to transportation and costs of transportation. Since then the construction of the Aswan Dam might at least go a long way to making this production aim a viable target. The Far East's basic physical resources and climatic changes and differences put the F.A.O. target for that area in serious doubt. And the Organisation's suggestion that Europe, North America and Oceania would be all right has turned out to be a forlorn hope.

'Production is soaring away from the rise in population in Europe. Production would be increasing at an even faster pace if it were not for marketing difficulties. Throughout most of Europe dietary levels are fairly satisfactory and population is expected to grow only by a modest 36 per cent. by the year 2000, or by 50 per cent if the Soviet Union is included.'

What the F.A.O. ignored, apart from destruction in Africa, was the destruction and birth problem elsewhere. Of course, the political institutions have not become more stable, and foreign aid – including as it does pesticides which harm the earth – may not have been the boon it was thought to be. The increases in population, the anxiety to bleed the earth of as much food as possible, the difficulties of transportation and marketing, the refusal or failure to trade between certain nations, plus climatic catastrophies, have all helped ensure that the Organisation's plan has largely remained a dream.

Shortly before he died, Lord Brockway, formerly Mr Fenner Brockway, the veteran Labour politician, outlined the problem in the *News of the World* thus: 'We must win the battle to save the starving. Two out of three people in the world will go hungry today. And tomorrow. And unless there is a drastic change in the battle to feed mankind, they will never know a day which gives them enough to eat. We all know the danger of the Bomb. Few understand the danger of World Hunger. But hunger may kill more than the Bomb. The population explosion may be more annihilating than a nuclear explosion.

'Already there are 300,000,000 in the world at starvation level. Two-thirds of the population do not get enough to eat. And each day there are 200,000 more mouths to feed. At present we are losing the battle. In the past year, the world population rose by 70,000,000 but there was no increase in food. There was, in

38

fact, an average of 2 per cent less for each individual on earth. The people of Asia, Africa and South America, the hungry people, did not eat as much in 1966 as in 1965. They will almost certainly eat still less in 1967.'

This is not a problem of temporary famine from unforeseen weather, such as the drought which has brought death to India. It is a permanent and worsening condition due to failure to grow enough food and maldistribution of the food which is grown.

The Food and Agricultural Organisation of the United Nations has prepared a report for the next 20 years. It lays emphasis on the need for more modernised production of food in the hungry regions of the earth and more mutual trade between the richer and poorer nations. Both are needed. Agriculture, particularly in Asia and Africa, is primitive. The absence of fertilisers and mechanical equipment is felt everywhere. There are inadequate measures against soil erosion.

The F.A.O. plan for the next 20 years is an advance, but it is woefully inadequate. While the report says rather optimistically that actual starvation could be ended by 1985, the admission is made that malnutrition (a polite word for hunger) would widely still persist. We need not only better production of food, but new spheres of production.

There are at present three largely untapped sources: the oceans, the jungles and the deserts. In all parts of the world, of course, men gather fish from the sea, but the effort is fragmentary compared with what it might be. Seven tenths of the planet is covered by oceans. 'In terms of sea food, we are still at the cave-man stage: we hunt, we do not husband,' Lord Ritchie-Calder has written.

He draws a dazzling picture of what might be done. 'We could have sea farms, sea-ranches, sea-pastures, sea-studfarms. We could breed not only fish but mammals like the dugong or sea-cow which is a substantial hunk of animal protein. We could fence off great sea inlets (some of them as big as Texas) by passing electric currents across the entrances – like the mild shock fencing which reminds animals not to stray. We could converts atolls into fish farms.

'There is also edible vegetation under the sea. The potentiality for food production is almost limitless. It is self-evident that the jungles could be food-producing. I am thinking not of the bush, though with water these could be made fertile, but the rich green extravagances of trees and undergrowth and creepers in Africa and Asia. They are a riot of watered fertility. Bulldoze them, clean them of stumps and roots, plough them with tractors and crops and they would grow almost overnight.

'More than one quarter of the earth's surface is arid and desert. This vast area, invading all the continents is unused by man except for the production of oil.

'It is now known that deserts can be made fertile. In Israel it has been proved that sand can be transformed by water into fruitful soil within three years. And under many of the deserts there are rivers and lakes.

'We have got our priorities wrong. We draw oil from the deserts: we leave the water. Water is now more important than oil. It could make the deserts blossom and save millions from hunger.

'This is not mere fancy. In America, Australia, Russia, Israel, and Africa, large areas of desert have been converted to trees and crops. But so far only a fringe has been touched. There is another opportunity. Research is now proceeding to desalinise sea water, but, except in oil-wealthy Kuwait, it is still too costly to operate. When we have added the water of the oceans to the water flowing across and under the deserts we shall have reached the stage where the wasted earth can provide food in abundance.

'The nations are spending millions on arms, fearing each other, while the danger mounts to human destruction more by hunger than by war.

'Only by a united effort of all the nations can we save the millions of lives which are threatened.'

Even allowing for honest hyperbole, there is no doubt about the essential truth of the problem. On the other hand, there is every reason to be cautious about the widely held belief that as much as two thirds of the population of the world is under fed.

F.A.O., Oxfam, Save the Children Fund and other activities have a vested interest in proving that the situation is very serious. Yet, even allowing for exaggeration in either direction, few can doubt that an unchecked population explosion can lead to a dangerous food shortage, starvation, and disease.

The idea that two-thirds of the world's people are undernourished originated after World War II when the ravages of war had disrupted the economies of several countries and food was certainly short.

Malnutrition still exists, particularly in India, Africa and South America, but what must be separated are the physical and human reasons for starvation. Bad land management and technical failure to transport food may have the same effect, but the cures for these ills are essentially different. It may be true that in a substantial number or most cases the countries are politically, and socially, incapable of gearing production and distribution of their own food resources. But no one can predict when food will be plentiful for all the future populations, nor when it will be able to reach them.

The following two tables are instructive. In the first, dealing with the growth of world food production, the increases in several foodstuffs are remarkable by any standards.

But, in fact, food production is not keeping pace with the rise in world population. The people of the world require more food at the rate of 3.9 per cent per year, but food production is, in fact, rising by only 2.6 per cent per year. Once again, though, the questions arise: Is the food being grown in the right places? Is it transportable? Are two thirds of the population undernourished as a result of the answers?

Take this example. In India only 2,500 calories per day are produced per cultivated acre, while Japan produces 13,000. Experts have ben known to suggest that fertilisers and water and the most productive of hybrid grains could redress this balance. After all India has five times as much acreage tilled as Japan. Unfortunately, the geographical situation does not permit such a simple solution. Japan grows lowland rice under

GROWTH OF WORLD FOOD PRODUCTION
(m. tons)

	1955–57 average	1962–64 average	1965	1966	1967*
Wheat	218.0	256.8	265.8	308.2	301.5
Coarse grains	414.4	481.0	500.1	528.5	536.7
Rice	215.3	252.3	254.6	255.2	282.3
Meat	52.19	64.96	68.07	71.12*	74.19
Beef and Veal	24.71	29.77	30.84	32.67*	33.70
Pigmeat	17.46	21.06	22.19	22.62*	23.72
Mutton and lamb	4.44	5.48	5.39	5.41	5.64
Poultry meat	5.58	8.65	9.65	10.42	11.13
Eggs†	11.02	13.65	14.32	14.67	15.39

* Estimate   † Excluding Communist countries in Asia
Source: United Nations: F.A.O. Commodity Review 1968

permanent wet conditions, while India relies on upland rice which is dependent on irrigation.

Moreover, the dependency on fertiliser and water in food production is the greatest obstacle in providing a European diet for the world. Neither water nor fertiliser can be provided in sufficient quantities, and the water supply of the world would run out before costly fertilisers could be supplied on a global scale.

The next table, although of 1966 origin, illustrates not only the low hectarage under fod production in some places but the height in others.

Readers will notice the high level of cultivated land, and potential production in Europe. If all the potentially arable land in this world was cultivated then there would be provided a high standard European diet for a population of 3,700,000,000 compared with today's total of 3,600,000,000. Unfortunately the projected world population for the year 2000 is 5,000,000,000. If we cannot feed those who are here how can we feed those who are to come?

Today, literally hundreds of millions of people are not properly or adequately fed, even by the dietary standards of the big British pigs that go to market. As there is bound to be an evergrowing food shortage, the dietary standards of some people must grow less.

What can be done? The F.A.O. believes that the solution is to be found in hybrid and synthetic foods. Hybrid rice and wheat are not unknown experiments, but neither are they not long term solutions.

Already, food tastes have been altered radically over a period of very few years, and the prospects of further, quicker and more drastic alteration are very real. As are the dangers, for hybrid grains are infinitely more prone to disease than natural grains. More than that, they swallow up fromthe ground far more rich nutrients than the traditional crop. To replace these nutrients more and more artificial fertilisers and pesticides are being employed. The dangers of this short-sighted policy will be seen in a later passage in this work. Here it is sufficient to note that many underdeveloped and emergent countries cannot

PRESENT UTILIZATION OF LAND AREA
(in million hectares)

	Total Land Area	Tilled	Pastures	Forest	Tilled, Pastures, Forest (%)	Other
Europe	493	151	91	138	77.1	113
U.S.S.R.	2,240	229	372	910	67.5	729
Asia	2,783	445	452	520	50.9	1,366
Africa	3,026	230	696	604	50.6	1,496
North, Central America	2,245	260	370	821	64.6	794
South America	1,783	76	414	940	80.2	353
Oceania	852	37	460	82	67.9	273
Total	13,422	1,428	2,855	4,015	61	5,124
Per cent.	100	10.6	21.3	29.9		38.2

Source: F.A.O. Yearbook, 1966

afford these expensive chemicals, and even when they are used they help destroy the natural soil fertility and natural insecticide properties of the earth.

Nor are artificial foods the real long-term answer.

It could rest with Mr F. R. Barker, chairman of the Oxford cattle marketing concern, who says: 'A diet of more meat and less drugs could enable us to recapture the strength and stamina of our forbears instead of being the strike riddled community that we are today.' More scientifically, however, the truth is that on the one hand intensive meat production as envisaged by the F.A.O. has both animal and mechanical limitations, and on the other factory farming has already proven to be a threat both to animal and human health. (Not to mention the cruelty alleged to be necessary in factory farming.)

The most boosted of the modern synthetic food formulae is the arrival of experiments to synthesise fats from coal, a process begun by Germans in World War II. They actually produced 2,000 tons of fat in one year. But quite apart from the undesirable taste and hygienic deficiency in the commodity the mathematical future of the idea is in doubt. It is costly and the amount of fuel required to produce a substantial amount of foodstuffs would be enormous.

All this may seem very academic to the isolationist and insular Briton.

Undernourished countries are not normally his concern, except in a humanitarian sense. If he looks at the global situation he will see how serious is the prospect ahead.

First, Britain is continually producing less food and importing more. According to 'The Changing Structure of Agriculture. Agricultural Departments in the United Kingdom, H.M.S.O.', the number of farms in the United Kingdom has fallen by 4,000 a year since 1963. In 1968 there were 200,000 full-time farms. About 40,000 large holdings now account for half the industry's output. The number of small holdings providing employment for only one or two men, fell from 96,000 to 84,000 between 1965 and 1968. In the same period their total output fell from 19 per cent. to 16 per cent.

At the same time farming, despite lavish subsidies, is not a worthwhile business, according to many farmers. The National Farmers Union claims there was a 13 per cent. fall in the average net income of farmers in the year ending March 1969. Many farm incomes, particularly in the arable sector, were below 1966 levels.

Since Britain is not a predominantly agricultural country, it is difficult to examine the island's position as an isolated unit. Rather should we see the West European situation as shown in this table:

Foodstuffs	Western Europe's share of World Imports (per cent.)
Frozen eggs	97.5
Oilseed cakes, meal	93.0
Bacon, ham	92.8
Fish oils	80.6
Oats	78.6
Poultry meat	78.0
Cheese, curd	77.3
Butter	77.0
Fish meal	72.7
Peanuts	71.6
Corn (maize)	68.8
Eggs	68.6
Meat	66.5
Wool	64.5
Barley	61.8
Copra	56.4
Meat extract	56.2
Sunflower seeds	54.6
Egg powder	54.5
Soybeans	53.5
Bran	52.8
Peas, Beans	51.6
Meat meal	44.4
Non-fat milk solids	44.0

Cottonseed	...	...	...	...	...	37.7
Sugar	...	...	...	...	...	28.6
Wheat	...	...	...	...	...	22.3

Source: Borgstrom, Georg. *Too Many*. (New York: Macmillan Co. 1969. p. 239.)

Western Europe will, because of the savage misuse of the land, and increased industrialisation, need to import more and more food. If the natural food production and distribution of the world cannot be greatly improved – and the signs are that it cannot – then the prediction is clear that there will be a very grave global food shortage before the end of the century.

the choking air

The yellow fog came creeping down
The bridges, till the houses' walls
Seemed changed to shadows, and St Paul's
Loomed like a bubble o'er the town
                      Oscar Wilde, Impression du Matin

As one who long in populous city pent
Where houses thick and sewers annoy the air,
Forth issuing on a summer's morn to breathe
Among the pleasant villages and farms
Adjoined, from each thing met conceives delight;
The smell of grain, or tended grass, or kine.
Or dairy, each rural sight, each rural sound.
         ... *Milton Paradise Lost*, Bk. ix. 1. 445

THE CRISIS we face may not be totally beyond mortal solution, but so far it appears to have been beyond the practical acknowledgement of politicians. True, they bounded into the 1970 General Election, which was bereft of popular issues, with some powerful thoughts on ecology. Even though it was on page 27 of a 30-page election manifesto the Conservative Government declared:

'Economic growth and technological innovation are the principal means of achieving a continuing improvement in our standard of living. But the effects of technological change can sometimes lead to a deterioration in the natural environment and in the quality of life. The public are rightly concerned about these dangers. We will improve the machinery of government for dealing with these problems. We will review existing legislation to ensure proper and sensible control in the future. The damage of the past must be repaired. The worst scars are in and around our industrial cities and towns. We will ensure that the natural beauty of our British countryside and seashore is conserved and wild life is allowed to flourish. We intend to launch a major campaign in which government, local authorities, and voluntary organisations will combine to produce a healthier, pleasanter Britain. We will vigorously pursue international agreements for the safeguarding and improvement of the environment. We will set clearly defined aims and target dates for the achievement of cleaner air and rivers, and for the clearance of derelict land.'

Then, before being elected, that Party had as its spokesman on the subject Mr Christopher Chataway, who in an article in the *News of the World*, said:

'Why should we live surrounded by filth, smells and noise? The roar of aeroplanes, the fumes from car exhausts, the stench from rivers used as open sewers, the tar-covered beaches, the slagheaps, the belching smoke, the great ugly pylons marching over open countryside – is all this bound to get worse?

Do we just have to accept these things as an inevitable part of "progress" in this technological wonderworld in which we live?

Quite suddenly these questions are being asked with a new insistence in Britain, America, and in Western Europe. Words like pollution and conservation are passing into everyday conversation. People are rebelling against living conditions that seem to be getting nastier, and Governments are being forced to listen. There is a yearning for cleaner, healthier, surroundings, and there is a growing fear, too – a fear that we may in our inventiveness, be unleashing forces that we do not fully understand. Thousands of sea birds die in the Irish Sea – perhaps from waste products of the plastics industry, but nobody can be sure. Persistent pesticides pass from one living organism to another and concentrations of DDT are found at the extremities of the world, even in the stomachs of pelicans in the Antarctic. Are these chemicals harmful to man? There is no evidence of it yet, but nobody really knows.

A growing volume of radiation waste from nuclear power stations, some of which will take more than a thousand years to decay, are buried with care underground or at sea. But how safe are these arrangements – in the case of earthquakes, for example? Again no one can really know.

In the years ahead we shall need a larger and more effectively co-ordinated research effort to pinpoint the risks in time. We shall need, too, tougher international agreements to deal with oil spillages, aircraft exhausts and noise and all those technological developments that may upset the delicate balances of nature. Already enough has been achieved in this country over the years to show that we can have a cleaner, more pleasant environment if we really want it.

As a result of the Clean Air Act of 1956, the London killer fog has been eliminated in the square mile of the City of London. 200,000 plants a year now bloom in several hundred varieties, where ten years ago only privet, laurel and plane trees grew. There have been real achievements too in cleaning up British rivers. In the 19th century, Parliament had sometimes to adjourn because of the stench from the Thames. Yet the other day a dolphin penetrated up the river as far as the Houses of Parliament – and lived to tell the tale. There is little sign though, despite all the talk, that we are making much progress at present in the battle against pollution.

Many rivers like the Irwell in Lancashire and the Trent in the Midlands are in a filthy condition. Many sewage works are increasingly overloaded yet the Ministry of Housing and Local Government discourage anti-pollution spending save in exceptional circumstances. As a result of the shortage of solid smokeless fuel, we are also going back on the clean air programme. Smokeless zoning is being suspended and Lord Robens, the Chairman of the National Coal Board, has warned that it is likely to be two years before progress can be resumed and new smoke-controlled areas declared.

The time has surely come to stop talking about pollution and to embark on a clearly defined clean-up campaign. As many young people up and down the country have already shown, it's a job in which volunteers can join. But the first essential is for the Government to set definite goals and target dates for the attainment of cleaner air and cleaner rivers, and for the clearance of derelict land.

Let us know by what date the laggard local authorities will be required to enforce clean air regulations and let us be certain that the smokeless fuel is then available. Let us determine to be rid of eyesores and the wasteland, and let us give priority to such schemes as that in London's Lea Valley which will turn derelict land into regional recreation parks for city dwellers. Let us set dates for the purification of all our rivers.

Of course it will cost money and take time. But if we have the will the 1970s can be the decade in which we start to restore England as a green and pleasant land.'

Such a statement by a leading politician might be expected to go unheeded after an election. Unfortunately Mr Chataway was not put in charge of pollution but was translated to the department of Posts and Telegraphs. Unfortunately, the problems he posed remain. Of all those problems, clean air is of primary importance.

Fourteen years have elapsed since the Clean Air Act of 1956 came into force, authorising smokeless zones, grants to householders to alter grates, but still the air is filthy.

The amount of poisonous sulphur dioxide polluting the air around London has probably increased in those years despite the Clean Air Act. A six-week testing of the air with a new invention shows that the City and Westminster are worst hit by sulphur dioxide.

The invisible gas has been associated with bronchitis and other respiratory diseases – although there is no direct evidence that it is a cause. But it is known that people suffer worst from bronchial and other diseases in areas where the air has a high sulphur dioxide content.

The new instrument for measuring the gas pollution was unveiled in London in June 1970. It enables scientists to keep a continuous check on the gas, instead of taking a 24-hour sample – the usual practice in Britain and abroad.

The instrument, perfected in Holland, will be marketed for £2,500 by Pye Unicam. It is wired into the ordinary telephone system so that when the sulphur dioxide content gets too high the message is recorded on a computer and a light flashes on a map pin-pointing the area or factory involved

In Britain, sulphur dioxide fumes are caused mainly by oil-fired central heating and smokeless coal – which are not banned by the Clean Air Act, and by those and other pollution devices in the twenty-three great areas which have yet to implement smokeless zoning.

Now Unicam want to see their machine installed throughout Britain, both at factories and at special observation points. A spokesman for the Government-run Warren Springs Laboratory at Stevenage, Herts. confirmed that the level of sulphur dioxide in the atmosphere had hardly changed since the Clean Air Act came into operation. But he said that in general the level of sulphur dioxide in Britain's air was decreasing very gradually – 'though not enough'.

Curiously, the air of London does not seem dirty. December sunshine in London has increased by 70 per cent in ten years as a result of smoke control, according to the London Boroughs Association.

Winter visibility is three times better than it was, says their report, and smoke concentrations have dropped by 80 per cent since 1958. Because of cleaner air, 138 types of birds can now be seen in London, compared with half that amount a decade ago. Most of these are typical 'town birds'. House martins abound. The quality and extent of plant life has also improved.

And, the report adds, since the winter of 1962/63 when the air was exceptionally contaminated, there has been very little evidence of any effect of pollution on death or disease.

Although there was no readily available information to show

that the likelihood of fog decreased as air pollution fell, there had been no major fog in London for seven years.

Not everybody shares this view. Dr Frank Taylor, a former president of the Institution of Heating and Ventilation Engineers is leading a team from the Institution which is carrying out a survey into the effects of sulphur dioxide pollution.

Pollution experts are worried that despite the Clean Air Act, the amount of sulphur dioxide does not appear to have diminished, and in fact, may be increasing. He says: 'It is my personal view that sulphur dioxide is the biggest single air pollution problem we have at the moment.' He reasons that since the Clean Air Act of 1956, the public has been complacent about air pollution, and almost unaware of the dangers of sulphur dioxide. This complacency has been caused by a massive optical illusion. The Clean Air Act rid London of its infamous smogs and now, to the man in the street, the air looks perfectly clean. But is it? Sulphur dioxide, in the concentrations found in the air, is invisible.

In certain areas the suspicion of the experts that SO_2, as it is known by its chemical formula, is still present in fairly heavy concentrations – has been confirmed, while other areas appear to be relatively free of sulphur dioxide pollution.

Air pollution is causing increased absence from work, according to a report (*Air Pollution and Health*, Royal College of Physicians) by a committee of the College on smoking and atmospheric pollution. The report said an analysis of medical certificates in Salford disclosed a doubling of sickness absence from bronchitis when concentrations of smoke in the air exceed a certain level. Records of admissions to London hospitals in 1955–6 had shown that the demand for beds for patients with acute diseases of the chest rose during peaks of air pollution and cold weather. Up to the late 30's death rates from bronchitis in middle-aged men and women had been falling. But since 1940, the death-rate from bronchitis in men had risen while the decline in the death-rate among women had been less marked. 'It is believed that these recent changes are due to increased cigarette smoking, which became more popular, among men particularly, during the first World-War and thereafter.'

Cigarette smokers, it said, were three times more likely to suffer from chronic bronchitis than were non-smokers. Cigarette smoking was also the most important of the causes of cancer in the lung.

But various studies indicated that when allowance was made for the effect of cigarette smoking, there remained a degree of association between deaths from lung cancer and the burning of solid fuels.

Just who pollutes the air? Uncontrolled industries in free zones are still responsible for much of the filth.

Airlines have been accused along with long distance lorries, private cars and ships which sail too close to shore. Gratifyingly, our pollution has attracted more anti-dirt campaigns than any other form of destruction. At the time of writing, a nationwide air pollution survey is being made by 8,000 university students. The students are making systematic measurements of air contamination by carbon monoxide, sulphur dioxide, carbon dioxide and ozone.

While working for spare-time degrees offered by the Open University, all students taking the first year science course, which starts in January, 1971, were being issued with home experiment kits for the pollution tests.

Dr Kenneth Mellanby, director of the Nature Conservancy experimental station at Monks Wood, Huntingdon, said 'We shall be getting a much more comprehensive research network than ever before to deal with air pollution. Up to now we have had to rely on around 200 people in the field to cover the whole of the country.'

At the same time two of the world's biggest oil companies, Gulf and British Petroleum, have disclosed developments which should help to cut air pollution. Gulf, which has spent over £6 million and thirty years of research to find a way of taking sulphur out of industrial fuels, has discovered a new refining process. Commercial-scale production has started. The result is expected to be a dramatic decrease in the emission of sulphur oxides to the atmosphere.

The process, by which the sulphur content is refined from 4 per cent. down to 1 per cent., was developed mainly in the

United States, but the first production plant has been set up in Japan, about 150 miles south west of Osaka. Details were released at a meeting of the Japan Petroleum Institute in Tokyo. (March 1970.)

Gulf is using the world's biggest oil tankers to supply the Bantry Bay terminal in Eire and is rapidly expanding its interests in Britain.

British Petroleum is ready to provide lead-free petrol 'as and when required'. The problem of reducing air pollution from cars rests on producing such petrol. Lead is used to give better mileage. But its presence makes it difficult for car designers to produce an exhaust system able to reduce carbon monoxide and hydrocarbon fumes.

Shell believe that petrol without lead could be produced fairly quickly, at increased cost, for cars with a compression ratio lower than that of existing models.

Yet much more needs to be done. British air is the foulest in Europe. Deaths due to bronchitis have been running at 10,111 a year in West Germany, 2,606 in France and 1,768 in Holland, the deaths in Britain for 1968 were 28,257.

It is essential that this disease source is fought at the earliest moment of pollution. The first global network for monitoring air pollution, set up by the World Health Organisation is about to begin.

London and Washington will be the international centres and regional centres will be in Moscow, Nagpur and Tokyo. Twenty other laboratories will be operating in various parts of the world. Reporting on pollution levels will make it possible to compare trends and to issue warnings where necessary. Sulphur dioxide and dust particles will be the substances most closely studied, but measurements will also be made of carbon dioxide and oxides of nitrogen.

To warn about dirty air is one thing, to prevent it is something totally different and nigh impossible. Early warning systems have been used for years to forecast natural phenomena such as storms, particularly of cyclonic force. People in the wake of such ferocities can take precautions, but cannot remove the source. An early prediction of smog belts can at least lead to drastic action at the origin of the pollution.

No town dweller today needs to be reminded of the atmospheric pollution caused by the combustion of coal, oil and petrol. Too many urban areas are overhung most of the time by a pall of smog whose more toxic compounds irritate the membranes of the eyes and respiratory system, produce cancer and otherwise shorten lives. Remember the deaths of 4,000 people in the London smog disaster of 1952.

The year 2000 will see a very highly industserialised Britain. To ensure it is a clean Britain then, far more will have to be done than hitherto. Despite the clean air policy, despite the statutory Clean Air Councils, despite the doubling of public expenditure on the subject, domestic coal fires remain the most evil form of air pollution. For the smoke which belches out of house chimneys, from two or three storey dwellings, hangs about at a lower level than factory smoke and consequently more people breathe and inhale it, aggravating the lung diseases they already have.

By 1970 only one quarter of the homes in Britain had been covered in fourteen years by the Clean Air Act of 1956. Only one in four homes were controlled so as to restrict the occupants to electricity, gas, oil, or solid smokeless fuels. There is some doubt about the reason for the lethargy in declaring more areas 'clean', the most common being that there is an overriding economic factor. The supply of smokeless fuel has been unduly short, while the demand for oil, gas and electricity heating has been restricted by the expense involved. Clearly the rate of progress to make Britain smokeless will have to be speeded if the twenty-first century is to be clean.

In the war against air pollution, as in so many fields, the issue turns on costs. The central government gives 40 per cent. and the local council 30 per cent. towards the cost of converting open domestic grates to take solid smokeless fuel. Because of the shortage, the Government has had to keep open unprofitable gas works and encourage the money-losing National Coal Board to produce briquettes made from anthracite to help out. So the cost to the taxpayer and ratepayer is quite considerable.

There is little doubt that the lack of money, either public or private, is responsible for the failure of industry to exercise similar control over smoke emission. Local councils have the power to act against industrial concerns over this nuisance, but there is a marked reluctance to do so, particularly because the vast majority of furnaces and chimneys are so very old that it would cost considerable sums of money to replace them with alternative kinds of energy. Many factory owners, if forced to stop their smoking chimneys, would be put out of business by the cost of conversion. As a result, local council inspectors prefer to use long term persuasion rather than short term prosecution to achieve a clean air policy around factories.

In time, conversions, the introduction of mechanically stoked solid fuel boilers, and limiting of smoke belches to the beginning and end of firing processes will help considerably. More important, though, is the research and development of devices which may well cleanse the smoke before it is emitted.

Not all the blame should be put on private industry, for it is a constant source of embarrassment to central and local government departments that they themselves are among the worst offenders against the clean air policy. Curbs on public spending have delayed the conversion or replacement of many public buildings which use antiquated heating systems. As a result these buildings, with their smoke-emitting boilers, seldom conform to the Government's own policies and laws. All the authorities can do, for the time being, is to ensure that new buildings comply with the legal requirements.

The next most important source of air pollution, though not necessarily third in density, is transport. It is also the most difficult to control, without adding markedly to the costs of research, adaptation and renewal. It is thought that if a limit was set on the amount of fumes a vehicle may emit, any device to comply with that limit might automatically produce a different kind of substance which would be equally obnoxious.

While the petrol engines give out more smell than danger through the exhaust systems, diesel engines are offensive on both counts. Therefore, the first move will be to lay down standards over the diesel engines, which will be comparatively easy. For petrol engines, considerable research will be required before alterations can be enforced by law. Cost of conversion to motorists is one problem, but it would be better if nuisances from private cars were looked at in the light of the future of that kind of vehicle.

Traffic problems are very much part of the environmental crisis, and the arguments for and against diesel engines, the steam Stirling engine, gas turbine and battery powered electric vehicles may well all be taken into account before there is an official move against the exhaust system of the internal combustion engine. The growing population and its demands for more and more private vehicles will make the problem more and more urgent, but whatever steps are taken to limit exhaust smoke they will have to be universally applied by giving public notice many years in advance of a change in what will be allowed on the roads. Meanwhile the research into the causes and effects of transport pollution, new measuring instruments to replace the visual checks on heavy vehicle smoke, and the content of such smoke must continue at increasing pace.

Perhaps greater than air pollution is pollution by noise. At least steps have been taken to combat dirty air, and although the working of legislation is slow, far more has been done by way of control than has been attempted or achieved against noise. Noise is a moving target.

By far the most persistent and annoying noises are those from aeroplanes and road vehicles. As the population has grown and more people have demanded cars and motor cycles, so the vehicles have become more powerful, and often power has meant noise. Even the action of the Government in regulating noise at manufacturer level, in April, 1970, has not had the desired effect. Even if the noise level of an individual vehicle is satisfactory – and we know that research has proved that a heavy lorry need not make more din than an average car – it does not solve the problem of many cars and many lorries all making a little noise together.

Short of a completely silent vehicle, with all the road accident dangers that would bring, the only practical answer would be to separate the heaviest traffic routes from homes and workplaces. And that would only be of benefit when good planning and industry has solved its own problem of removing the cacophony from the work benches and assembly lines.

In modern living, the noises from aircraft are clearly more vexatious than those from land traffic, and despite attempts to control it the sound has become worse. The larger, the faster the jet airliner demanded for commercial aviation, the greater the thunder. At the time of writing the Concorde is still being tested by running at supersonic speeds down the west country corridor reserved for it, breaking the sound barrier, while scientists measure its effect on such ancient buildings as the 12th century St. David's Cathedral, in Wales, and farmers and gardeners watch for the glass in their greenhouses and conservatories to break.

This shattering threat of more powerful aircraft does not seem to be deterred by the powers of the Board of Trade to tell the British Airports Authority to reduce the noise of aircraft using their facilities. The Authority is required to demand maintenance of height on approach of aircraft; minimum noise routes after take-off; prior approval before a new type of aircraft is allowed to operate at an airport; aircraft to reach 1,000 feet before build-up areas and then throttle back; imposition of monitored noise limits after take-off, lower by night than by day; and severe restrictions on night jet movements at Heathrow London Airport. One wonders which, if any of these powers, are exercised, particularly in mid-summer when holiday air traffic is at its height. During the course of producing this work, the author saw, in the early hours, on two occasions, from the west carriageway of Regents Park, and from Dulwich Village, both central London areas, jet airliners flying under 1,000 feet. Moreover there is no traceable record of any official criticism, rebuke or other action against those responsible.

At the present rate of advancement to quieter aircraft, there is little doubt who is winning the battle of noise and power versus silence. The law has been changed by the Public Health (Recurring Nuisances) Act of 1969 because abatement notices could not be served on noise makers unless they were actually making it at the moment of service. The Civil Aviation Act of 1968 enables the President of the Board of Trade to deal with airport management problems, including noise. The Air Navigation (Noise Certification) Order was meant to foreshadow even international action against the menace, reckoned to limit sound by half. And above all that, the Ministry of Technology spends £1,250,000 a year on aircraft noise research.

Yet, the Concorde aircraft, the silver hope of the British aircraft industry, is a supersonic jet airliner, which registers noise at a level beyond anything previously known, so loud that it requires special air corridors, and special regulations appertaining to its type alone. And despite its expense, despite its Anglo-French co-ordination in development, it is unlikely to ever be a commercial success, and what is described as the technological spin-off profit—even this will be undermined if something cannot be found to cut its infernal ear-shattering effects.

the dirty rivers, the foul sea

> And all of the waters that were in the river were
> turned to blood and the fish that was in the river
> died; and the river stank, and the Egyptians could
> not drink of the water of the river.
>
> *. . . The Bible, Exodus*, ch. 7.

BRITAIN HAS some of the filthiest rivers in Europe.

If you have sat on an oily or otherwise dirtied south coast beach, or tried to fish an exhausted river, you will know something about water pollution.

Britain is surrounded and criss-crossed by dirty water. In addition to the coastal districts, Britain has 20,000 miles of rivers and one in every four is polluted. One in every 20 is so contaminated that it scarcely warrants the word river.

The worst are so fouled with industrial waste and sewage that even the loglouse, the lowest form of river life, cannot survive in them.

But a clean-up campaign cannot start because an 'urgent' survey, ordered more than a year ago, has not been completed. The survey began in December, 1968, when housing minister Mr Anthony Greenwood asked local authorities for details of their river pollution so he could plan a clean-up programme. Many authorities have not replied.

Meanwhile experts warn that pollution may be getting worse. Most of these dirty rivers – including the Thames where salmon were caught 100 years ago – provide drinking water as well as drainage. The River Thame in Notts. is coal black from china effluent, and the Yorkshire Calders copper-coloured with a white detergent head.

It will cost £30 million to clean the Tyne and £50 million for the Trent.

A survey was taken of the ten worst rivers in England and Wales, based on the amount of oxygen dissolved in the water – the formula used by experts to measure river pollution.

1. The Beam in Essex
2. The Irwell at Manchester and Salford
3. The Tame at Lea Marston, Warwicks
4. The Rother at Woodhouse Mill, nr Sheffield
5. The Mersey at Warrington, Lancs.
6. The Trent at Nottingham
7. The Calder at Wakefield
8. The Don at Doncaster
9. The Aire at Beale, nr Pontefract
10. The Roding at Redbridge, Essex.

For the record, the cleanest major river in England is the Derwent at Stamford Bridge.

Go to the seaside and you will discover that every day, millions of gallons of crude sewage are pumped into our seas and all tidal rivers and estuaries. That includes human waste and anything that can be flushed down a lavatory. Every day, firms and nationalised undertakings pour their industrial waste into the same waters. No one knows how much there is, where it comes from, what it contains or where it goes to.

Adding to the sea's unofficial role as Britain's dustbin are the refineries and tankers which cause oil slicks and the Government – which allows the dumping of military gases and chemicals and the disposal of radioactive waste.

It's not a health risk to swim in raw sewage, according to a report by the Medical Research Council which was published eleven years ago, but the hidden horror is who can trace a disease to one single dip in the briny?

At least two-thirds of the local councils which pipe sewage into the sea do not treat it in any way. Most of them make sure that sewage is piped at least a mile off the shore, but unusual tide or wind conditions can wash it back to the beach.

Seaside resorts near every river and estuary are continually fighting against domestic and industrial waste landing on their shores. The River Thames swills 500,000,000 gallons of sewage every day into the estuary.

The Tees regularly carries untreated discharges. The Humber carries a thousand tons of sulphuric acid waste every day.

The truth is that water which has been contaminated by sewage can carry many diseases – such as typhoid, polio, hepatitis and dysentery. It is time for an up-to-date examination of the dangers in the sea. Of course sewage should not be discharged where it can be seen or washed back to the beach. Two miles off shore should be the minimum limit for the pipeline.

Once the sea and rivers are polluted, the cleansing process is both difficult and costly. A recent estimate put the cost of purifying a four-mile stretch of the River Tyne in excess of £30,000,000. Remembering that 5,000 miles of Britain's rivers are polluted and 1,000 near to sewer standards, the total cost would be out of the question.

The size of the problem can be gauged from the years and decades we have permitted the fouling up of waterways.

Up till 1830 it was possible to catch a salmon in the Thames at Chelsea Bridge. Record year was 1820, when the catch was the biggest ever. Then came industrial development and the angler's scourge, pollution. Now I hear that over 200 of the rivers of this country are unfishable for the very same reason.

The upper Severn where thousands of fish from salmon to eel have been poisoned by pollution has been forecast as useless. From the source to the estuary reports of dying fish have become as regular as were once the reports of record catches.

Then came the start of the fight against the stream and tide of overwhelming pollution. In 1963 thousands of farmers and country householders throughout Britain faced the possibility of prosecution and a fine of £100 as a result of river pollution regulations which came into force. Under the new law, anyone discharging effluent into a stream or ditch had to have the permission of the local river board. If they had not already applied for consent they could be prosecuted, and fined on summary conviction a maximum of £100. Once permission had been sought applicants were to be protected from prosecution until a decision on their case was reached.

Unfortunately, the penalties were by modern standards too low. Besides, many river boards reported that many thousands failed to send in application forms.

In Devon, when the first 1,000 applications were received, officials estimated that about 18,000 people in the country were affected by the new regulations.

The position was similar in other agricultural areas. Norfolk River Board sent out 8,000 forms, but only about 1,300 were returned. Essex River Board received only about 300.

Although thousands of people have been committing an offence, few prosecutions have taken place. One river board official said lamely, 'We shall try to be as lenient as possible and not to prosecute unless absolutely forced to do so. We know who the worst offenders are, and if they have not sent in their applications we shall send them a letter warning them of the position.'

The River Boards' Association commented: 'The general rule is to exercise the art of persuasion. A river board would never dream of prosecuting except in a bad case where someone appears determined to defy the law.'

So much for the new anti-pollution drive. The law had been passed in 1951 but only operated from 1963. The reasoning seemed to be that rivers had been used for centuries to carry away waste from homes, factories and other forms of industry. A few more years would not make much difference, and what more could be done anyway?

Standards for preventing the pollution of rivers were inevitably a compromise. The only complete solution would be to treat everything that is to be emptied into a river until it is as clean as the water it is to join.

Scientifically this would nowadays be possible. In practice, it would be far too expensive. As cities and industries expand, sewage works become overloaded. A new plant may cost several million pounds and takes two years to build. Local authorities had a mere £40,000,000 on loan from the Government to build new works. One works alone would cost more than that.

Technically, by law, nothing poisonous must be sent into a river. Domestic sewage must be previously treated, although the standards of treatment vary according to the plant available. Water used in various industrial processes, such as washing coal, electroplating, the manufacture of textiles and paper, must also be pre-treated to clean it before it is discharged. But so far regulations have not been sufficient to prevent large stretches of rivers becoming polluted.

Much depends on what standards the river boards enforce under the new Act, and how far standards generally can gradually be raised. Yet if persuasion and warning fails how else can the foul process be stopped?

The cleanliness of a river depends on the minute amount of oxygen dissolved in the water. A really clean river contains ten parts of oxygen to a million parts of water. No fish can live in water that has less than 3.3 parts per million.

Oxygen is essential for the bacteria which gradually break down and cleanse all refuse and waste in the river. Just as they break down the contents of a garden compost heap. They use up oxygen as they work ; if no more is available they cannot continue the cleansing process and the river becomes heavily polluted. Water can take up a small amount of oxygen from the air on its surface ; water plants and water-weed also give out some oxygen. But when heated water from power stations or industrial plant flows into the river, the amount of oxygen is reduced.

Hot weather, too, cuts down the oxygen available. Fish have died by the thousand in the lake of St. James's Park, London, during a heat wave. A river becomes really black and evil-smelling when no oxygen is available.

Fish cannot live in the Thames where it passes through London. The oxygen content of the water at Westminster Bridge in summer is only 1–2 parts per million.

But generally, when the oxygen content of a river is reduced, the fish are not killed immediately but are able to move upstream to healthier stretches. When large numbers of fish are found floating dead on the surface of a river, it is usually because some poisonous substance has been allowed to escape. Factories have been prosecuted for letting this happen.

The Government's Water Pollution Research Laboratory maintain that the length of British rivers where fish can live has actually increased in the last five years.

Regulations applying to the upper stretches of rivers have only been extended to tidal estuaries since 1960. The estuary of the Thames extends sixty miles from Southend, through London to the first weir at Teddington. The Mersey estuary, running through Liverpool to Warrington, is twenty-nine miles long.

It was assumed for centuries that any waste discharged into an estuary would be quickly swept out to sea. But experiments in the fifties proved definitely that tides take pollution upstream as well as towards the sea. Waste introduced into the Thames at Teddington took from two weeks to two months to reach the sea.

Even now, standards demanded for heavily populated estuaries are often lower than for the rest of the river because of the expense that would be involved by higher standards.

It has been calculated that it would cost £21,000,000 to get the Thames clean enough for fish to live in between London Bridge and Tilbury.

With the stinking sea and scabrous rivers, polluted by an inflated population which is seeking more food, the prospects for the model year of A.D. 2000 reach new alarming proportions. And leading the question table: Where will we obtain our water from?

Industry, having polluted the potential water supply needed for industry, the people are left to ponder on the source of their own drinking water. To begin with, the vast underground supplies of water purified for drinking have been consumed, and the Greater London Area depends on rivers for 25 per cent. of its supplies. And since much of the country's water supplies already contain various chemicals, said to be dangerous or potentially dangerous, the existing situation has its own concern.

For the future, there is the fact that Britons consume 25,000,000 gallons per day, while the total rainfall in this country is only 50,000,000 gallons per day. And, at the present rate of increase, the consumption may well rise to 60–70,000,000 gallons per day. How then can the rivers, at the tremendous cost indicated, be purified to provide water for industry and water for everyday consumption?

Unless the cost is made a matter of governmental concern, and perhaps water is transported from coastal areas to the central cities, a standstill in industry and drought conditions for the population, with all that entails, cannot be ruled out of the question. For to remove an essential source of energy from industry, and food from mouths, by failure to provide or by pollution, must rank as one of the greatest scandals in the history of mankind. Yet even as we speak about the dirtiness of seas and rivers, science tells us that we must look more and more to the oceans for the provision of our daily food.

The annual takeout from the seas of the world has risen more than twelve-fold since the start of the century and will continue to rise at much the same rate until the next begins. But it is not in the capacity of nature to provide inexhaustible supplies of anything, and there are already signs that the rich harvests of the seas are losing their natural ability to provide for ever fish as food. One estimate is that the rise in fish food from the seas from 5,000,000 metric tons in 1900, 64,000,000 in 1970, could never exceed 150,000,000.

Evidence of the decline in marine food production has already been shown in the industry which has resorted to inland fish nurseries and breeding grounds. As the tide of pollution continues the very food on which the fish depend is running short. It is all very well to talk about the algae on which fish feed, but it requires considerable quantities of algae to feed just one fish.

Even if fish is found in new waters, there must be taken into account the transportation availability and costs. At the same time, those fish will be dependent on the naturally rich wetlands around our coasts, the very wetlands which are now suffering from chemicals, pesticides, oil slicks and rubbish disposal.

Marine nations, with their multifarious islands, depend very much more on fish food than countries which are part of the greater landmasses. The Japanese, for instance, depend on fish for more than half the protein content of their foodstuffs, while

Britons are content with little more than one-tenth. At the rate seas and oceans are being turned into non-producing deserts, we will find that first our fish is becoming less in standard and we may well reach a stage within thirty years when fish becomes too unpalatable to be a viable daily food.

The Baltic and the Black Sea have already been marked as biologically 'dead' for commercial fishery purposes, and the large number of fishing vessels engaged in pirating fish from the territorial waters of other lands is a clear sign of the industry's plight. The end of the century may, in the fishing world, be too far ahead to be used as a reliable gauge of fish produce, but man would be foolish indeed if he did not heed the warning of the French oceanographer, diver and marine biologist Cousteau. He believes the oceans of the world will be dead, from a fish producing point of view, within one decade, not three.

What are we doing about it? Britain, for ever insular, and seldom financially able to enter into the international projects of such things as oceans, might do better than merely look at her own rivers. Just because it is something like a century since the Houses of Parliament had to adjourn because of the pong from the River Thames, there is no room for complacency. There will always be those who will argue about the cleanliness or otherwise of our waterways, but it does not profit us if the oceans die. We can, to some extent, render pollutants harmless, purify sewage treatments, and regulate the floor of polluted rivers to retain the oxygen in them. But we cannot was our hands of the matter at the river estuaries knowing that there is more pollution in the seas and oceans beyond.

Of course, we must look to our own rivers first. We need the water and we need it pure. If we do not ensure that, we can, by the year 2000, suffer a drought unknown in these islands. The quantity of liquid waste discharged into public sewers now reckoned to be 70 per cent of the total, is rising. Within thirty years the total volume of effluent will certainly double.

So as long as we need drinking water for human consumption we must at a very much larger rate increase our purification plant and treat our waterways as a source of ultimate drinking water and not merely as streams to be prettified. Whatever is done to our present rivers, it is essential to note the estimate that as many reservoirs will be needed in the next thirty years as in the past century. It has been suggested by the Government that some old storage reservoirs can be converted for this purpose but it is certain that there are not sufficient of these to meet the estimated demand.

Whether or not the required reservoirs can be found is problemmatical, and even if it is solved, the whole question of purification may founder on financial grounds. For a series of economic crises has held back ordinary expansion and construction of sewerage and sewage disposal works, while little or nothing has been done for the positive purification of rivers. During the six years up to 1970, capital expenditure which has been permitted has risen by 40 per cent, while the cost of schemes which would have been put in hand has been incalculable. Now that both central government and local authorities are aware of the problem, they are discussing grants in terms of a few millions. Hundreds of millions may be required, since ultra modern technology has produced some schemes for approval which may require as much as £35,000,000 each.

What can we do about sea and beach pollution? Although the amount of industrial and natural effluent which reaches bathing areas of the seas is comparatively small it is increasing and the seas are not boundless. Tides return the bulk of what does pollute to the beaches which are provided by nature for people's enjoyment. If we don't prevent the 17,000,000 tons of domestic refuse dumped every year (including its increasing tonnage) from polluting first rivers, then the seas, we will not have a chance of stopping the worst sea pollution from adding its dreadful effects. Oil is a major evil in the world of pollution.

Ever since the tanker Torrey Canyon smashed on the Southwest shore rocks of these islands, and discharged oil which polluted many beaches, ruined several resorts, and killed many sea birds, we have been well aware of the dangers. A series of measures have been adopted. The Inter-Governmental Maritime Consultative Organisation (I.M.C.O.) has produced a number of conventions, including one which lays down regulations covering oil discharged into the sea. The North Sea, English Channel and much of the North Atlantic are prohibited areas to oil dumpers, although one would not appreciate that fact by the amount of sands dirtied, clothes ruined, and birds with their feathers matted by such wastes. Nations are co-operating in tracking oil slicks. The oil industry and tanker owners are contributing to compensation funds for people who suffer from oil pollution. And the penalty to be meted out to tanker skippers who wrongfully discharge oil in the sea is being increased from a £1,000 maximum fine on summary conviction to £5,000. And the Ministry of Technology, with an army of petroleum inspectors, keeps watch on the oil exploration off our shores in case of discharge by mishap.

Yet as the hunt for oil continues, and more oil slicks are spotted, and still more oil fouls the beaches around Britain's coasts, can we be really satisfied? Discharges continue both in and out of prohibited areas and still reach the shores. And the quantity is increasing, while the methods of breaking up the oil slicks are primitive, and the damage becomes infinitely greater. The tanker owners themselves accept that one incident could cost them in compensation as much as £4,200,000.

Add to rubbish, sewage and oil, then the threat from chemical and radioactive wastes. The natural source of ionising radiation has been increased first by the use of nuclear weapons and later by the use of nuclear power in industry. It is true that the level of radiation to which a human being can be exposed without danger is known and control over such a modern waste which is a pollutant is strict. It was essential to control it from the outset, and the partial ban on testing nuclear weapons plus the round-the-clock monitoring of radioactivity at nuclear power plants has been commendable.

The danger occurs, however, in the following: Small radioactive waste may still be leaked into rivers or the sea. Solid wastes are still dumped in canisters to the ocean beds. And even while it is thought that this is well within the bounds of safety, there must be some apprehension, for the full effects of radioactivity on human beings is not known. Much of the work concerning chemical and radioactive materials is controlled by the Ministry of Defence, subject to rigorous security. It is known that when people working on such materials have become ill, the fact that they are subject to the Official Secrets Act, as civil servants, has been invoked. To the mysteries of their illnesses must be added the enforced silence of their protests and the diagnoses of their medical advisers.

Stories of such illnesses continue to leak out, particularly in the region of chemical and biological warfare experimental stations. Some of the tales bear the marks of hysteria and ordinary anti-war propaganda, which, though often laudable, does not help us understand the problem already cloaked in secrecy. It may be salutary that the Government has only once prosecuted anybody for disposing of radioactive waste in an unauthorised and therefore potentially dangerous manner, but what the mind does not know about such dangers the hand can hardly prevent. Nor have we been helped by the open knowledge that the Government itself has been guilty of dumping nerve gas canisters, found off the Isle of Wight, and that no one has been able to explain the chemical reaction found on birds and other sea life dying around our coasts.

If we are content to accept that everything is being done to limit or prevent disasters to life from chemical, biological and radioactive forces, we must ponder the thought whether the secrecy imposed adds or detracts from that contentment.

Chapter Six

the derelict land

Ill.fares the land, to hastening ills a prey,
Where wealth accumulates, and men decay.
. . Oliver Goldsmith, *The Deserted Village*, 1.51.

PRINCE PHILIP in the book 'Animal pictures of the World' summed up the depredation of the country by saying:

'There is every sort of thing wrong with our environment. Practically everyone has a personal experience of some form of pollution in the air, of the soil or in water, if only as oil on the beaches.'

Waste and derelict land is there to be seen by anyone who cares to look. Pylons and motorways blaze across the country, and every year more land disappears under housing estates, factory buildings and reservoirs. None of this is deliberate, it is simply the outcome of a rapidly growing population becoming increasingly more prosperous, enjoying longer periods of leisure and making full use of all the discoveries of science and the opportunities of technology.

Not surprisingly the combination of all these factors is having an appreciable effect upon our natural surroundings and the question which needs to be asked is whether we are satisfied that these effects are all in the best long-term interest of the human population and the surroundings in which it lives on this earth.

Unfortunately the answer is not a simple one. For instance it is quite easy to justify the use of certain pesticides on the basis that the extra food is needed by the starving populations of the world. But is this justification entirely valid if the long-term side-effects of those pesticides destroy whole populations of wild creatures and in the end threaten the health of more people than they save? The difficulty about conservation of nature or of anything else, is that it is always a choice between what is desirable from an economic, material and practical point of view.

Judgement on the former is on a severely practical basis, judgement in the latter depends upon intellectual and conceptional standards and this is what makes compromise so difficult and challenging.

It is easy to make decisions if you only know one side of the case, but to be uncompromising is to risk being dreadfully wrong. This obvious need to compromise between development and conservation in nature has reached a critical point. It is true that the lesson has been learned in a small way, as for instance, in the statutory close seasons for game and fish. It was quite obvious that unlimited exploitation in the long run would wipe out the wild stock. Today this danger applies to everything in our surroundings. Unlimited exploitation for leisure just as much as for profit can ruin not just one feature of our natural surroundings but the lot.

Conservation is not a matter of trying to stop every development or an attempt to make the country into some sort of museum. It is a matter of setting limits, of creating a desirable environment and of finding acceptable compromise. Certain major issues flare up now and again and the debate rages with great heat but once it's over, interest is liable to disappear just as suddenly.

Somehow or other we have got to learn that what looks like the cheapest and most obvious solution today may turn out to be a vastly expensive mistake in a few years' time. If either collectively or individually, we approach the problems of conservation from the standpoint that 'I'm all right Jack', then our generation will come to be loathed and despised by all who come after us till the end of time.

In Paris, on February 8th, 1970, as reported in *The*

Times, Prince Philip, continuing his interest in conservation, declared:

'Drastic political action to protect the natural resources of Europe was demanded today by the Duke of Edinburgh at the opening ceremony of the European conservation conference in Strasbourg.

'After sketching the "crisis situation" created by the pollution and destruction of man's natural environment, the Duke laid stress on what must be done first before necessary decisions were taken.

' "We need to create an administrative system which is capable of formulating a sensible and comprehensive conservation policy, which can take preferably the right decisions and which can eventually carry the policy and decisions into effect." Some aspects of conservation he said, could be dealt with by advice and encouragement, while others would require legislative action and international controls.

'What should not be disguised was that this policy was "going to cost a great deal of money, and the denser human population becomes, the more expensive it will be. The destruction of wildlife cannot be reversed. We cannot postpone the decisions any longer." The time for discussing present mistakes and future dangers were past, since "we now know enough to put many things right. We also know quite enough to be able to say in which direction research programmes should be aimed." Such programmes should not be allowed to become excuses for doing nothing else. "Research and action must go on at the same time." The Duke continued: "It is just as well to recognise that any measure taken o protect our environment will be unpopular in some quarters, and will inevitably cut across national boundaries. Above all, the conference must not be satisfied with words. "If no one is capable of taking any action it will be a waste of time and effort to establish even the most brilliant advisory body if there is no wa yof putting its advice into effect. "This conference," the Duke concluded, "will mean nothing at all if it does not lead to practical conservation measures in every country. All its discussions and resolutions will disappear into the polluted atmosphere if it does not produce more closely organised co-operation between responsible and effective government departments.

' "All the impatient speeches will be so much effluence under the bridge if they are not followed by drastic political action." The theme of the conference, which has been organised by the Council of Europe to launch European Conservation Year 1970, is "the management of the environment in tomorrow's Europe". M. Jacques Duhamel, the French Minister of Agriculture, emphasised that the co-ordination of methods of conservation was above all a question of political will. For a start, he made three proposals.

'The creation of a European fund to fight pollution – to be used in serious cases such as the poisoning of an international river; a European diploma in ecology; and a competition in primary schools for nature conservancy posters.

'None of these proposals would require much political effort to carry out, but the nettle proffered by another speaker, Prince Albert of Liege, would be more difficult to grasp. "There are reasonable targets for progress," the Prince said. "But it is no longer healthy to accept the infernal race for economic growth. If he wants his species to survive, man must limit his appetites." This is where political will will really be necessary, for in order to preserve their natural resources effectively nations will have to accept a limit on their economic growth rates and co-operations on their profits.'

If there is anyone in doubt, that uncertainty can be quickly dispelled by a glance at the countryside. This green and pleasant land, about which we sang and recited as children, has been the subject of many changes, some subtle, some not.

The most apparent to the eye is the gradual disappearance of hedges and trees.

More than one thousand years ago the countryman planted trees first to mark parish boundaries, then to enclose private lands, and inevitably to bank the roadways of rural Britain. Yet today the miles upon miles of hedgerows are disappearing, particularly in Eastern England. The Council for the Preservation of Rural England estimate that 5,000 miles of hedges disappear each year, which means that by the year 2000 one quarter of the 600,000 miles of hedgerows (estimated in 1960) will have gone. That is if the rate of destruction remains at the same level. Advancement demands that more of this greenery goes.

The reason for the destruction is to be found in farming economy. Ours is the land of the small farmer, but his numbers are dwindling, and the farmer who replaces him wants a bigger farm. At the same time – and it is the basic reason for the change – the days of the horse who could plough no more than a five-acre field and then needed the shade of tree and hedgerow are gone forever. In place of the horse comes the mechanical animal which does not require hedge limitation. So down come the hedges, the destroyers forgetting that there is more in a hedgerow than a mere boundary fence or a windshield.

Farmers will insist that there is no evil in this destruction of a deliberate nature, but who can explain away the disappearance of the birds who find insect food and nests in the hedges? This destruction is done in the name of progress. In the name of beauty and conservation it should be reversed, but presumably if we must have the food to feed our inflated population we must improve our farming methods and in the process lose our beautiful countryside and much of the wildlife with it.

Some economists, rather than scientists, have indicated that globally it would be possible to meet the food demand from the greatly increased population by doubling the area now under cultivation or in pasture. And this can be done by the wholesale levelling of the world's forests. They forget that forests collect water for the soil and prevent erosion of the earth. One has just to look at the barren hills of the Mediterranean and Aegean, which were once lush and fertile, to see what gargantuan destruction can do to the earth. As if the economists should not know that deserts and wastelands which once, in 1900, formed one-tenth of the world's surface now occupy one-fifth.

Chop down the trees, remove the natural water storage, and the earth around loses its nutrient value. With it goes the wood which is still the basic fuel for millions of homes, and, in paper form, provides newspapers and books to educate and communicate between people. And these commodities are not being spurned; on the contrary, the demand for these products increases yearly. So much so that land under afforestation will have to increase by 75 per cent. to meet that demand by the end of the century. This is, of course, impracticable. The chop has replaced the planting for so long the forests can never recover.

In Britain, the Forestry Commission works on the principle that a tree has no commercial value until it has been planted for a quarter of a century, and that the real return does not come for between fifty and sixty years. Which means that, in 1970, we have already decided what will happen to our forestry position at the end of the century.

The Commission's plantations have mostly been only planted since 1950, and its operations are very much a balance between preservation and production. Every year the Commission plants hundreds of thousands of trees, but looks as much to the thousands of forest and woodland visitors as to the arrival of the axemen. Officially, the Commission is charged with the task of granting access to forests, and with the conservation of wildlife, but it must also pay heed to the finances of timber.

Britain spends £650,000,000 annually on importing timber and wood products from the decimated forests of the world, while at the home-front a domestic production of ten per cent. of the nation's needs is being rapidly increased to twenty per cent. When one considers this expenditure is the fourth largest item on the national shopping bill, one can understand the temptation to step up the supplies in order to save foreign currency and help the balance of payments. But unless a close check is made on the balance between conservation and national, natural need Britain's timberlands will join the growing desert lands of the world.

Forestry, like the rest of agriculture, is declining. Farming people have fallen from 980,000 in 1947 to 450,000 in 1968, a drop of more than fifty per cent. And as the land decreases in quality and yield, with fewer workers production will inevitably decrease. The Forestry Commission's labour force is also decreasing and at the latest count the total was a mere 7,348, made up of 2,892 in England, 2,945 in Scotland (including 1,377 in the crofting counties) and 1,511 in Wales.

Now open land is being reduced at an alarming rate. Incursions into green belts round our cities continue. If the farmer removes his trees and hedges the Forestry Commission cannot stop him. On the contrary, the Ministry of Agriculture and Fisheries give grants for the removal of such obstacles to good farming. (The definition of good is expansion, but like most matters which come under the heading of expansion or improvement they are short term.) So we find that the countryside as we know it is being depleted of its natural greenery. That deprivation affects the soil on which we depend for food as we have already read.

And on top of that all the land available for agriculture is also being depleted. The current estimate is that there are about 30,000,000 acres of cultivable land. One six-hundredth of that land, some 50,000 acres, is lost to city development every year. If that rate remains static, which is doubtful, the loss by the end of the century would be a massive 1,500,000 acres.

Yet that is not all the harm that man can do to his own land.

Bleeding the earth of its goodness and greenery has not been enough. The world has been over-mining as well as undermining itself. It has been estimated that, taking 1967 as a standard, the world will by the end of the century need thirteen times as much aluminium, nine times as much copper, seven times as much iron, and eleven times as much lead. Each individual industry must know if this production is possible, and, although the returns appear to be beyond their forecasting ability, it appears to be beyond the resources of the earth to supply such largesse. Even allowing for the argument that forecasts can be based only on what present technology could produce, it seems unreasonable to expect those needs to be satisfied.

One has only to look around at the collapse of mining in Britain to understand the probabilities.

Miners have offered themselves and been used as political ammunition for years. Remember the battle cries to the electorate? 'You have never had cheap coal, only cheap miners! Nothing has been more pitiful in industrial Britain than the social and economic plight of these people. The love-on-the-dole book ; film and political speech ended in a better deal for

78

miners, nationalising the industry, but no one seemed, to think about the future. If the miners received a better deal, why worry about their long-term future? The truth is that the betterment of miners came too late. They had already taken their sons into the pits, and those sons have been faced, and are still facing redundancy. One by one the mine shafts have been sealed. Even Barnsley, capital of the coal kingdom, has lost its last pit.

True, the number of pit closures has varied. There were only forty in 1969 compared with seventy in 1968, when 57,200 men left the coal industry.

It was expected that closures in 1969 would involve from 30,000 to 35,000 miners. Although the figure was well below the previous year's total it did not mean that the National Coal Board had made a sudden reduction in the number of collieries to be shut down this year. The high level of closures in 1968 was due to the Government's decision in the final quarter of 1967 to defer the shutting down of sixteen pits, because of the swollen level of unemployment then. This decision was rescinded and the sixteen pits were closed in addition to those already planned for the year.

It was estimated that coal production in 1969 would total 155m. tons of which 7m. tons would be from open-cast and licensed mines. The 1968 output of 164·1m. tons was 8m. tons lower than in 1967.

Both the then Prime Minister, Mr Wilson, and Lord Roben's Chairman of the Board, seemed for ever anxious in pointing out that mines were closing at a lower rate, and that miners were leaving in a slower exodus. In March, 1969, the Prime Minister said: 'In the last four months the outflow of manpower from the coal industry was running at the rate of 32,500 a year, which was well within a manageable figure of rundown.' The Coal Board had said that it can manage a rundown of 35,000 a year.

Consider the figures. There are in the mining industry nearly 400,000 employees, made up of 344,030 mine workers, 27,078 overmen, deputies, and shift workers. At that rate of reduction, all the mines would be empty and closed by 1983.

At the same time as pits close and miners leave the industry, the pits still open meet 53·6 per cent. of the nation's energy needs. And they reveal that demand for coal is growing.

The truth is that the industry has never been planned, and availability of coal, labour and technological progress have never gone hand in hand. As a result it is uneconomic to keep pits open, and between 1970 and 1975 more than 120 collieries will have to be closed. This means that the number of mines will drop below 200 compared with the 320 working in April, 1969.

If that forecast proves to be correct the labour force would be cut to 143,000 from its 1969 level of 319,000.

As in many cases of social and industrial collapse, the solutions are temporary and make-shift. At the time of writing, it is proposed that the Government should give the Coal Board a 30s.-a-man-per-week premium to keep open pits threatened by closure.

But the cash should go to the pits where there are more people out of work rather than those where labour is scarce.

The payment, proposed by M.P.s, is that payment of a premium, analogous to the Regional Employment Premium, could delay the closure of mines in development areas.

As Iain Mikardo, Labour M.P. for Poplar and chairman of the M.P.'s Committee on nationalised industries, put it, 'We are not intending that the premium should be used artificially to maintain production of coal which cannot be sold. It would be used marginally to influence whether a pit in a development area should be closed later than some other pit in a more prosperous part of the country.'

All of which is to put off the evil day as long as possible.

Detailed solution of the mining industry's problems seem impossible, without direction or encouragement of labour. If the pits are to remain open and meet national needs then the labour and technological forces must go together where the coal is.

It follows that when, between October, 1964, and March, 1970, 268 collieries have been closed or merged, and the labour force cut from 488,800 to 296,700, they will leave behind a scenic void. The collieries close but the spoilheaps linger on.

The *Yorkshire Post* revealed that an average of four collieries a year are ceasing production on the Yorkshire coalfield, but no systematic scheme for eliminating the spoilheaps left behind. The West Riding Planning Department in Wakefield has more than enough dereliction to keep them going already. Recently closed pits receive no special priority. In fact they are often less unsightly than the ones which closed down many years ago. But the problem is most acute in South Yorkshire, where both closures and reclamation schemes are concentrated. Work in this area has been helped by the Government's decision last year to designate it an intermediate development area. This means that reclamation schemes approved by Whitehall qualify for a 75 per cent. grant – and not just 50 per cent., as it was previously.

But all eleven of the collieries which have closed in the past six years, there are no firm plans to eradicate dereliction and camouflage the pitheaps. This is the case at Wharncliffe-Silkstone, Wharncliffe-Woodmoor, Nunnery, Altofts, Monk Bretton, Snydale, Denaby Main, Hemsworth, Netherton, Barnsley Main and Thorne collieries. A total of twenty-five Yorkshire pits have been closed since 1964.

Special priority has been given to spoilheaps along the M1 corridor and dereliction along the route of the proposed M62 is to be given a new look quickly, too. At Whitewood, near Castleford, derelict land there is to be reclaimed as part of a £1m. scheme to establish a new industrial site.

Note how the master concrete road appears to be the deciding factor in clearing such spoiled areas.

Put all those scenes together and we can visualise a picture of the year 2000 in which the countryside is defaced, not only with the disused winding gear pockmarking the horizon, but with a blackened earth and the shells of homes and outbuildings marring the land. We do not have to wait for the end of the century for the signs. County Durham already has villages where industries have closed, and the old men sit at their doors, in a silence left by the young people who have gone elsewhere, with their children, to find work. Multiply those villages across the counties and the canvas will be one of complete desolation.

81

Awareness is not the same as solution. If we take 55,000 acres of agricultural land for urban development each year, and suffer further losses on moorland and hill country, and take the 120,000,000 tons of sand and gravel from the earth each year, we have the basic problem. If we then cover the land with solid wastes from homes, farms and factories with chemicals, with the noxious substances from domestic and industrial chimneys, and let other noxious substances descend from the air in wind and rain, we will require all the self will, regulations and laws to prevent such a catastrophe long before the end of the century.

When man first produced pesticides, he knew they must be poisonous to be effective. He could not foresee that he would not be able to control them and that they would harm other living matter than those he chose as his target. First the insecticides aldrin, dieldrin and heptachlor had to be withdrawn from spring seeds because they were killing wild life, then DDT was discovered to have biological effects on the area where it was used. Fertiliser with its high content of nitrogen was found to wash away in rain and cause an overgrowth of weed and algae until the nitrate poisoned the rivers and the 'blooms' outgrew the crops it was meant to help.

Man, in his anxiety to make livestock fatter and healthier, introduced antibiotics which gave the animals a resistance to bacteria, a resistance which has prevented those animals from giving the serum and vaccine needed to treat man's own illnesses.

Man has made his own bed of pollution on the land and as long as he lives off that land he will have to lie on it.

the beastless jungle

Hunting was the labour of the savages of North
America, but the amusement of the gentlemen of
England.
  ... Johnson, *Johnsoniana.*

IF WE accept that man has got his priorities wrong, what are we
to make of his attitude towards world wildlife. Anti-pollution,
and anti-destruction and all their allied subjects have not provided anything like as much popular support and practical help
as the preservation of world wild life.

In this field a second royal figure has taken a lead. Prince
Philip was one. Then in 1967, Prince Bernhard of the Nether-
lands opened the international congress of the World Wildlife
Fund.

The Prince had the aim to reach a world agreement with an
inter-governmenal conference to handle the subject. He named
1970 as the 'year of nature reservation.'

Mr Peter Scott, the distinguished painter and ornithologist,
first vice-president of the fund, had made the point that not
animals, but human beings, formed the biggest obstacle for the
preservation of nature. The Torrey Canyon disaster, which
fouled Britain's South coast with oil, and the destruction by
means of chemical products of a jungle area in Vietnam had
all made this abundantly clear. To combat such evils the fund
declared a conservation quinquennium from 1968 to 1972,
which the World Wildlife Fund would help to sponsor.

The fund was pioneering an important, hitherto neglected

aspect of human progress – the proper care of the human environment on an earth of finite size with a massive human population increase.

Since then the World Wildlife Fund, 'The modern Noah's Ark,' made good progress in establishing itself on an international scale in the public mind, as boasted in the first report.

'An unexpectedly wide interest in and sympathy with tne idea of saving wild life and wild places has been amply demonstrated,' said the report, which covered the fund's first three years, up to the end of 1964. Through national appeals £675,000 had been raised. Sums varied from an anonymous £100,000 to countless small gifts from all age groups.

The world target for the fund 'dedicated to its concept that the conservation of nature is for the long-term benefit of humanity,' is £1,500,000 a year. Administrative costs have been kept to a minimum.

The international trustees dealt with 145 international project applications, of which 126 were approved in principle. Of those, thirty-nine had been completed, seven were in progress and seventy-seven were grant-aided in order of priority as funds became available.

Mr Scott, who edited the report, said that future generations would have good cause to revile us if through carelessness and lack of foresight we destroyed the natural world which was their rightful inheritance. Human interest must prevail where there is an unavoidable collision between survival of man and survival of wild life, he adds. But such conditions are rare and in nearly all cases a little thought and ingenuity can permit coexistence of man and wild life, without which man is much poorer.

To the question whether there is room to feed the ever-increasing human population and at the same time provide adequate space for wild life, he gave an unequivocal 'yes'. He pointed out that more than 1,000 kinds of animals are in danger of becoming extinct at the hands of man.

But still remains the problem of trying to persuade governments to undertake nature conservation on a far wider scale than at present.

Funds are far short of what is needed although private individuals have been generous. Officials at headquarters of the fund here estimate that about £2m. a year has to be spent to save more than 1,000 species and races of animals and birds in danger of becoming extinct. In four and a half years' work the fund, which operates with the International Union for the Conservation of Nature, has expended no more than £500,000 on some seventy projects.

Extermination continues to increase, economic development is changing the face of areas which used to be safe for wild life. Chemicals, both in the form of industrial effluent and agricultural pesticides are taking heavy toll of flora and fauna.

Of the 200 or so kinds of mammals and birds that have disappeared since the beginning of the Christian era, 70 per cent. have gone during the past century and 40 per cent. in the past fifty years. This is why the fund has declared a state of emergency.

An example of the danger of extermination is provided in the Guadalquivir marshes, on the south-west coast of Spain, where land reclamation is going on rapidly at the expense of the fauna for which the delta was formerly a sure refuge.

The fund has intervened to ensure that a substantial section of this wilderness, which is a living place or staging post for a large range of animals and birds, will be preserved as the Coto Donana Nature Reserve. After long negotiations with three landowners, the fund bought twenty-five square miles at the end of 1964 at a cost of more than £100,000. Three-quarters of this sum was provided, as an interest free loan, by an anonymous Swiss helper.

In June last year, the new reserve was handed over to the Spanish Government, which is now responsible for its preservation and the upkeep of a biological research station. The fund is now negotiating to acquire an adjoining area but success depends on support from the European public.

At present money comes in through national appeals in six countries: the United Kingdom, the United States, Switzerland, Holland, West Germany, and Austria. Other appeals are to be launched soon.

Parallel with the Coto Donana project, the fund has been able to rent, as a first step, 1,100 acres of the Seewinkel region of Austria, to the east of the Neusiedlersee and near the frontier with Hungary. This wilderness of marshland and primitive steppe is also threatened by reclamation.

Although the Coto Donana is the largest project yet undertaken by the fund, most of its long-range undertakings are in south-east Asia, Central and Latin America, and in Africa. One of the first grants made was of £20,000 for a white rhinoceros conservation and anti-poaching campaign in Uganda, then newly independent. The rhinoceros was being killed in large numbers because powder made from its horn was believed to be an aphrodisiac. By 1960 the local population had been reduced to under 100 and the fund intervened just in time. One may be excused for thinking that such great energies used for preserving world wild life might be better expended on conservation at home. But the wider, global problem is not only a more dramatic and appalling dilemma, it has certain object lessons in the study of environmental problems and cannot be divorced from the more domestic perils. Witness the whales.

Today the blue whale is threatened through wholesale slaughter by the whaling fleets of Japan, the Soviet Union, and Norway. Unless a lower whaling quota could be fixed and enforced, there was a danger that all breeds of Antarctic whales might become extinct in a few years. The whaling quota agreed on and announced by the International Whaling Commission last month was not, as they claimed, an effective conservation plan but was nearly twice as high as the figure agreed on by scientists. The commission, in fixing this quota, were discounting the advice of their own scientists who had come to the conclusion that the quota should be fixed at 2,000 blue whale units, with an absolute maximum of 2,500. The figure agreed on by representatives of the commission's thirteen members nations was 4,500 blue whale units.

Whalers have been ignoring the scientists' warnings not because they disbelieved them, but people will not pay any attention to what the scientists say because they want to get as much out of the whales as possible before the industry collapses.

Whales are a valuable source of food and income and the present slaughter is an almost unbelievable piece of short-sightedness. People at the top of the industry are making sure, by refusing to cut down the crop, that there will very soon be no whaling industry at all – perhaps in as short a time as three years.

The World Wildlife Fund, the International Union for Conservation of Nature and the Fauna Preservation Society as a result have asked for quotas 'which will immediately call a halt in the decline of Antarctic whale stocks and start the long process of restoring them to a level at which the maximum yield can be sustained'. The figure they suggest is 2,000. Otherwise by the year 2000 the figure could be nil.

Prince Philip, following one of his globetrotting tours, discovered that the kangaroo was also a prime target for destruction, after an estimated 60 tons of kangaroo meat was being processed weekly in Australia, a lot of it for pet food. This meant that every week about 10,000 kangaroos were being killed. And, he declared, 'This can't go on much longer before some of the rarer kinds are exterminated. As it is, the toolach wallaby was completely exterminated in the 1920s because it had such a valuable pelt.'

Protection came too late to save the passenger pigeon and only just in time for the buffalo.

Evolution was not the cause. Man was responsible in three ways: by destroying the natural habitat of animals; through 'indiscriminate' commercial exploitation of them; and by 'indiscriminate' fishing and shooting for sport. 'The trouble is that it is all quite indiscriminate, unintentional, as if in a fit of absent-mindedness.'

For if Britain has little control over evolution, it is certainly doubtful, on this evidence, whether we can control our own even involuntary actions.

What more can man kill? The British pet lover's 'greed' for exotic animals is threatening to kill off a species of tortoise, according to zoologist Michael Lambert.

About 300,000 tortoises are imported from Morocco every

year. They are sold for 12s. each in pet shops. The shepherds, who collect them as babies in the Moroccan hills, get 6d. each for them.

Mr Lambert estimates that up to 1,800 tortoises a day are transported to Britain during the summer. They arrive in sacks, roasting on the steel decks of the cargo ships. Sailors spray the creatures with salt water to cool them. Many soon died because of the climate.

Complaining to the Royal Society for the Prevention of Cruelty to Animals has indeed beneficial effects, but they are by nature post-beneficial. Mass purchase, mass transit, can only have the effect of overcrowding in pet shops, and it has long been more than a suspicion that less than scruplous pet-dealers overcrowd such pets so that children will take pity and buy them.

There has been a deliberate delay in referring to the big game hunting effect on wildlife. One could hardly do better than refer the reader to Mr Guy Mountford's book 'The Vanished Jungle' (Collins, 1970). One of Britain's leading ornithologists and conservationists, he took part in the two World Wildlife Fund expeditions of 1966 and 1967 which he so vividly recounts.

According to the author the members of the expeditions found that the losses of wildlife were much greater than they had anticipated. One of the most threatened species was the Royal Bengal Tiger. Small wonder when one can find reliable statistics to show that just two of Indian's maharajahs each killed well over one thousand tigers. Today the total population in East Pakistan is only 50–100. Also in Pakistan the leopard has declined 90 per cent in fifty years and is in grave danger of extinction.

Again the fund has scored by getting new legislation introduced in Pakistan to protect endangered animal species, and this has led to the creation of several protected reserves and two national parks. Thus many of the animals which have been brought to the verge of extinction will be saved.

The most reliable estimate is that there are some 800 species of birds and mammals in danger of extinction in the world today. They include seven species of tiger, seven of leopard, fifteen of lemur, six of squirrel, eight of whale, seven of bear, four of otter, nine of seal, five of wild ass, five of rhino.

Populations of rare animals include the Orang-outang, 5,000; Mountain Gorilla, no less than 500 ; Pygmy Chimpanzee, unknown ; Asiatic Lion, 162 ; Florida Cougar, less than 100 ; Ceylon Elephant, 1,000–1,500 ; Kouprey, 200 ; Aye-Aye, not more than fifty ; European Bison, 790–800 ; Black Lechwe, 4,500 ; Arabian Oryx, less than 200 ; Sand Gazelle, 'greatly diminished' ; and Pyrenean Ibex, perhaps 200.

In addition we may not at the end of the century see four species of kestrel ; fourteen of pheasant ; eight of owl ; or eight of woodpecker. The short-tailed albatross is down to forty-seven, and there are less than 100 monkey-eating eagles.

This alarming catalogue can be added to in greater detail. There were 40,000 tigers in India in 1930, now there are only about 2,000–2,500. An expert has recently reported that in approximately three years' time there will be no tigers living in the wild in India. The world population of tigers is now about 2,500–3,000.

Before the Second World War there were approximately 30,000–40,000 blue whales, now the world total is somewhere between 630 and 1,950.

The United States pet trade is responsible for the killing of probably half a million parrots in the Amazonian basin per year ; this provides 10,000 live specimens by the time they arrive in the U.S.A.

Twenty-five different species of primate will soon be in danger of extinction as a result of the need for providing specimens used in scientific experiments. In 1967, 1,500–2,700 chimpanzees were killed to enable the United States to import 400 of them.

In Chad 90 per cent. of the addax and scimitar-horned oryx have been shot in the past twenty years, mostly by oil men. (This represents 10,000 addax and 40,000 oryx.)

In the United States in 1968 15,236,000 fish died as a result of water pollution.

In fact, every year in the present century at least one animal has become extinct. Two hundred species of animals have disappeared in the last twenty centuries, 38 per cent. of which have become extinct in the last fifty years. Small wonder when we learn of such wholesale slaughter as that of 200,000 ocelots and 20,000 jaguars annually in the forest areas of South America.

Let us look more closely at two species. First, the tiger. He is a beast who does not command sympathy and there may be only 600 left in the world. After the gun, man has, just in the past two decades, found yet two more powerful weapons against the tiger: jeeps and pesticides. Unscrupulous hunters, greedy for skin money, set off in jeeps at night, gunning down everything unfortunate enough to come into the headlights. Folidol, a pesticide easily bought and even distributed free to farmers, is an even quicker way to a rich prize. Poisoned meat is left along the tiger's beat, and death is quick and excrutiating.

Out of the seven recognised races of tiger, six of them are listed in the Red Data Book published by the International Union for the Conservation of Nature, which means that they are all animals in danger of extinction.

The tiger exists in an area from the Caucasas to Sumatra. The Siberian tiger is the largest and inhabits the remotest parts of Manchuria, Russia and Korea. It is estimated there are about a hundred in Russia and China, and fifty in Korea. In Russia and Korea they are given full protection.

The Caspian tiger lives in northern Iran, Afghanistan and Russia. There are perhaps sixty or ninety left in Iran and Russia together, where they are protected. There is little information on the Chinese tiger. It is hunted indiscriminately as its habitat is occupied by human development, although it probably still exists in Central, Eastern and Southern China. Reporters believe it is quite rare.

It is thought that there may be about twelve Javan tigers existing in the Betiri Forest Reserve in East Java, but the number is often put at three or four.

While it might still live in northern parts and mountainous regions, there are no figures available on the Sumatran tiger.

The Bali tiger is probably extinct though the figure has sometimes been put at two or three.

These figures give us a total of 255. Adding an arbitrary twenty for the Chinese, makes it 275 for the six endangered species. We are then beyond the Red Data Book into the realm of the Bengal tiger which once ruled the forest of India, Pakistan and Nepal. Here estimates vary widely. Some opinions stand out: Jim Corbett, whose memory as a hunter of man-eaters and as a naturalist is venerated across India, estimated 2,000 in 1961. Mr B. Seshadri, writer of 'The Twilight of India's Wildlife', however, gives 2,800 in 1969 – although he admits taking into account an old saying amongst jungle people: 'For every tiger you see, at least five see you.' Other researchers state firmly that 600 is an optimistic maximum total for all tigers, everywhere.

These are honest differences amongst people working in a very complex field. But there is no need to wait until the Bengal tiger too, is pinpointed by a Red Data statistic.

For, meanwhile, the destruction of Caspian forest areas to grow cotton and other crops has driven the tiger into even remoter regions. The Siberian tiger also suffers from the decrease in the once-great forests of Manchuria, and subsequent decline of deer, boar, and other prey. Reserves and sanctuaries, understaffed and poorly supported, are poached, and some species are not yet protected by law.

Realising that the tiger needs only privacy and food, The World Wildlife Fund is helping to create reserves in Nepal and Pakistan. At present WWF is concerned with four sanctuaries.

The Chitawan Wildlife Sanctuary in Nepal, which is 120 square miles, is extremely rich in wildlife and affords the protection to many species other than the tiger – leopard, elephant, spotted deer, black bear – and is one of the last sanctuaries of the Great Indian Rhinoceros. The sanctuary was cleared of all settlement and about 4,000 people were moved and resettled.

For the special protection of the tiger, two new sanctuaries are being planned.

The Karnali sanctuary in central West Nepal has many advantages such as dense forest and grassland and an abundance of the tiger's prey.

The Sukla Phuta area encloses swamp, dry grassland, and stretches of heavy forest.

In Pakistan, the Sunderbans tidal jungle at the delta of the Ganges and the Brahmaputra offers particularly suitable areas to be set aside for the protection of the tiger. It is hoped that the existing small reserve will be enlarged to 300 square miles for this purpose. There are important opportunities for developing the new reserve as a tourist attraction, as there are many river tributaries which penetrate into the jungle and provide a means of seeing the animals, and several hundred species of colourful birds, at quite close quarters.

The tiger is capable of adapting itself to a wide range of temperatures; it is at home in temperatures as low as minus 30°F in Manchuria as well as in the hottest parts of tropical Savannahs. It should not be too difficult to preserve an animal as adaptable as this. Let us give Jim Corbett the last word:

'The tiger is a large-hearted gentleman with boundless courage, and when he is exterminated, as exterminated he will be unless public opinion rallies to his support, India will be the poorer by having lost the finest of her fauna.'

Let us look next at the polar bear.

Here is an animal which still tempts the hunter, but one is entitled to ask – as the World Wildlife Funds has asked:

'Will men be able to bring even the polar bear to bay?' It hardly seems possible, when we consider the bear's advantages. He lives in the most uninhabitable, desolate free area left in the world. He seems to be unbound by territory, a drifter on ice floes some 200 miles off land, ranging anywhere within the Arctic Circle and as much as 800 miles below it, solitary and self contained. He is an expert swimmer and diver, quite at home in the water far from the sight of land. And yet on land he can move with catlike agility, far outrun a man on the level and do better than that through rocks or broken ice. With deadly accuracy, modern hunting methods and the decline in his staff of life – the seal – have landed the polar bear, all 950 average pounds of him, solidly into the Red Data Book of Endangered Species.

Other circumstances are contributing to his plight – for one thing, during the past 100 years the ice of the Arctic Circle has begun to melt – not due to any fault of man as far as we know. The Arctic becomes less and less remote to men: explorers, geologists, prospectors, researchers, and even inspectors, all are trespassing more and more frequently into what was once a solitary domain. With some exceptions, these are petty offenders, however, most likely to admire and leave the rightful ruler to his business. There is one type of trespasser who does not: the rich, trigger-happy hooligan, come to bag his bearskin.

'Jet Set Stalks Polar Bear' ran a *Sunday Express* headline not long ago. The story brought conservationists' blood to a fast boil. 'Get-away-from-it-all' sportsmen will be paying £200 a week to stay in stone huts near an Eskimo settlement on the Hudson Bay. From the settlement they set out in jeeps through the tundra to look for summer-foraging bears. Canadian law permits only Eskimos to shoot the bears, so officially the Jetsetters watch their Eskimo guides do the shooting. Unofficially of course, one can guess what happens. When the hunting is good, the guests will enjoy a steak or two with a real difference. The taste? Experts say: 'It's delicious, but a little fishy'.

From Oslo, well-heeled thrill-seekers have been able to go on 'Arctic Hunting Expeditions' to the Norwegian islands around Spitsbergen, taking their trophies from the security of ice-breaking cabin-cruisers. Alaskan 'safaris' set out in pairs of light planes, one to herd the prey into the sights of high powered rifles in the other. 'Can nothing be done?' comes a vehement chorus of wildlife friends. Something is being done, we can answer, and with a great deal of luck, it may be just not too late. Legal protection is of course the key, laws that have teeth, laws that give full protection. But protecting polar bears is made difficult by the bear's own farflung wandering. To convince the governments conservationists have needed facts, and since the bear respects no national boundaries, international co-operation was needed. Such things happen with ponderous slowness.

At last in January, 1968, a polar bear group was founded under the wings of the I.U.C.N. – the International Union for the Conservation of Nature and Natural Resources, which publishes the Red Data Book. Five nations can count the polar bear as a resource: the U.S.S.R., U.S.A., Canada, Norway, and Denmark (for Greenland). Each has two scientists working in the group.

The research that is being done is quite fascinating. A Canadian zoologist spent the dark Arctic spring of 1968 poking into the dens of hibernating mothers and cubs. He found that the temperature within these lairs may be as much as 37°F above that outdoors. Cubs, usually twins, are born in an almost larval state, the size of rats, blind, deaf, and helpless for the first month.

Another polar bear expert, who works for the American University of Maryland, has been working on tracking bears by satellite. He and his colleagues have attached transmitter-carrying collars to some 50 bears, whose movements were being charted by a N.A.S.A. satellite.

Thor Larsen, of the University of Oslo, leader of a research team working at Spitsbergen, reported to W.W.F. last autumn that seventeen bears had been recovered or re-sighted, out of 103 tagged. Two of the recovered ones had migrated across the North Atlantic along the East Greenland Coast around Cape Farewell. The team is trying to establish whether several groups or only one large breeding population of polar bears exist in the Arctic, a question of high importance for management and conservation.

The Polar Bear Group, at its February, 1970, meeting, announced that a total of 450 bears have been tagged by the teams of its member nations and that there are roughly five identifiable polar bear populations. These are located in: (1) the Spitsbergen–Franz Joseph Land – east Greenland region, (2) the Hudson Bay region of Canada, (3) the high Canadian Arctic, (4) the high Canada – eastern Alaska region, and (5) the western Alaska – eastern U.S.S.R. region.

The Group's research will continue, especially focusing on how these populations move and breed and where they den.

Heat sensitive scanners aboard aircraft will be pressed into census-taking service. The Canadian team will begin work on a statistical model, studying the correlation between polar bear numbers and movements, ice movements, seal distributions, and other factors.

All members stated concern about the dangers of possible oil spills, off-shore drilling, and other increasing economic activity. The market for polar bear hides is increasing, says the report.

Until the figures are in, and the migration maps complete, we who work to throw up defences will have to use estimates. How many polar bears are there now? Ten thousand, at the maximum, says Dr Uspenski, eminent Soviet scientist.

Official 'harvesting' figures give about 1,500 per year being killed, a reasonable 15 per cent one might think. So why shouldn't people who can pay for it have a little fun? Why shouldn't the tourist industry and thereby the government in taxes, take their profits? Such rationalisations ignore the life pattern of the animal. Polar bears are solitary giants, only taking an interest in each other in the short March to May pairing season. Most important is the fact that the female is only able to reproduce every two or three years. With a shrinking population, so that the bears just don't find each other at the right time, a shrinking habitat, and new diseases brought by man's animals, the birth-death ratio is not at a healthy balance. And the scales tip further and further against him with every year hunting is permitted to take its needless toll. The World Wildlife Fund is giving every encouragement to the Polar Bear Group and several National Appeals have donated generously to support the research work at Spitsbergen.

There is some consolation in the fact that the bear is quite adaptable and some 1,000 are living in zoos, where they often become fat and playful, breed, and live to a decent age. In a wild state this adaptability means that he travels further and further south as the seal fails him more often, and comes more naturally into the sights of high-powered rifles.

The King of the Arctic can no longer be spared for a setting for the traditional baby picture, nor to provide a conversation piece for the bored and affluent. Those governments whose responsibility it is should follow the fine example set by the U.S.S.R. and give full protection to one of their most majestic resources.

After reading what man has done to our international heritage – and is trying to do to the elusive polar bear, one cannot but be ashamed at what man in Britain has done to his own puny, by comparison, wildlife.

Among the species which have become rare and are threatened here are the pine marten, polecat, dormouse, mouse-eared bat, otter (in danger only in the south and east), and sand lizard.

The list may be small but British wild things are being pushed nearer and nearer the edge of disaster. In this time of environmental crisis, it is wild plants and animals that give way first, as their homes in the forests, hedges, marshlands and sand dunes are destroyed, and natural balances knocked helter-skelter. Slowly we are waking up to the realisation that when wild things can no longer survive the omens are gloomy for man as well.

While all those rural acres are going into urban development there are only some 334,000 acres of nature reserves in Britain. This represents a tiny percentage of our total land area – less than 1 per cent.

The World Wildlife Fund, among its many efforts, contributed £20,000 from 1962 to 1968 to county naturalist trusts to help with the purchase of 5,000 acres of reserves. This is a gallant effort but if we do not, or cannot, move more quickly, then the nature reserves of Britain in the year 2000 will be barely existent and those which do exist may have little or no wild life to inhabit them.

the unmanageable city

To cities and to courts repair,
Flattery and falsehood flourish there;
There all thy wretched arts employ,
Where riches triumph over joy,
Where passions do with interest barter,
And Hymen holds by Mammon's charter;
Where truth by point of law is parried,
And knaves and prudes are six times married.

> . . . Prior, *The Turtle and the Sparrow*. 1. 432.

I live not in myself, but I become
Portion of that around me; and to me
High mountains are a feeling, but the hum
Of human cities torture.

> . . . Byron, *Childe Harold*. Canto iii. st 72.

WHILE THE nation overbreeds, and faces underfeeding, and man destroys the countryside, he has by no means been more considerate towards his cities. He continues to choose that Britain should be an urban a not a rural world. The Romans in the time of Caesar Augustus were only 10 per cent urbanites. The United States of America today is all of 60 per cent urban. And Britain is even more so. And when men get together in closely knit conurbations to compete for land, for buildings, for families, for schools, for hospitals, for jobs and for profits it is inevitable that, unchecked, they will damage their own environment.

The vast sprawl of adjoining and overlapping areas for human activity that make up what we are pleased to call cities and

97

towns has no real policy of containment or expansion which can be for the good of the residents. Name one township which can boast a policy which ensures that the evils described in this book do not take place. Not one? No, not one. For it has become natural to conduct urban affairs on a competitive rather than a coordinative basis.

At the top of the pyramid is the central government, which, by handing out grants determines much of the local government activity. This is meant to ensure, in its way, that national policies, as approved by Parliament, which is the supreme authority, are carried out nationally. But it is neither administratively practical, or locally possible, to treat all areas exactly alike. The central government, therefore, tends to act in a permissive manner towards localities. Its attitude is: If you put forward a scheme within this framework, or according to that model, we will see if we approve it and whether it is eligible for a grant from central funds. Central government experts will insist that they do not have enough control over localities, while local government experts insist that there is far too much bureaucratic interference from the central authority. We shall see which is true.

One of the principal functions the centre allows the county to do on its behalf is to build roads. Just look at your rate demand, and, if it is set out in the modern informative method, you will see that of all costs burdened on you as ratepayers 'highways' are the most costly. The county tells the borough where the roads will be built and what must be paid for them. Small wonder that roads, as the railways have always done, rule our lives. No matter whom we elect to local, county or central government, the demand, always described as a need, for roads is ever present.

Julius Caesar ordained that all goods should be brought into Rome by night because commercial traffic so congested the narrow streets – remember, the Appian Way was less than twenty feet wide – that the citizens could not go about their business or pleasure. The night air was therefore constantly disturbed by the noises of animals and carts, and the cursing of those who drove them. The demand, or need, for roads after

2,000 years has not diminished, nor have the demands for commercial traffic to move by night, or on restricted roads. The only addition has been to suggest that private vehicles be banned from city centres.

While the demand continues for motor vehicles by private persons (who want them more and more as status symbols rather than as a means for travelling to B from A) the demand for road space must increase. And as long as the county rules the roads, and licenses the vehicles, the demand will continue to be met. Similarly, as long as the county is the responsible authority for highways and housing, and the borough only for housing, highways will have priority over homes. Of course homes must have roads with accesses to them, but there is an ever growing priority for cars 1; roads 2; and homes 3. The acquisitive society has been largely responsible for the development of that priority for many Britons pay more atention to their status car than to their homes, and there must be a substantial number of people wo pay out more on cars, by way of hire-purchase instalments, maintenance and running costs, than they do on their homes. The picture of a gleaming limousine at the kerbside, a colour television in the living room, and a leaky roof over the home – often subsidised by the ratepayer or by an overburdened landlady – is one of modern Britain.

It must not be assumed that only public development is bad for the environment. Public works tend to have a priority in the public eye, and because they are answerable to the public, receive a larger proportion of criticism and exposé. But the borough authorities tend to mask and hide the private developers to an extraordinary degree.

Democracy demands that we elect worthies to our town councils, and despite the enlightenment of the public over the years, and the bridging of the gap between rich and poor, and between public and private minded people, the businessman is still the dominant worthy in town affairs. When businessman meets businessman, even as fellow aldermen and councillors, there is a degree of understanding and rapport which permeates, if it does not transcend, their public works and duties.

There is no accusation of regular, perpetual or large scale

corruption, but it must be obvious that there is a large degree of cameraderie among our town fathers which makes pure public service virtually impossible. The law demands that any member of a council should declare his interest if he has a business interest in any subject under debate. The law also ensures that public works carried out under contract should be tendered for in open competition, and that the tenders, giving such details as price and time to complete, should be delivered to council officials (not members) and placed in a sealed box and opened together. The most advantageous tender to the public is then accepted on the vote of members.

But while no businessman-cum-town councillor can offer better terms, having seen his competitors' terms, there is an unfortunate situation by which he tends to escape the controlling powers of the local authorities. Take here the issue of pollution.

We have not moved far from the days when gentlemen walked on the outside of ladies because the inhabitants of London emptied their slops from the overhanging upper floor windows on to the pedestrians below. We still have town dwellers who empty their garbage into streams which flow through their fellow citizens' lands, and we have factories whose effluvia ruin nearby beaches and creeks.

If a local businessman-cum-councillor is responsible for such dumping, do we really expect that his fellow businessmen-cum-councillors will prosecute him? It is open for his opponents to report him, to demand that his anti-social behaviour stop, or to move for a prosecution. But the fact is that very few town worthies, whatever their political views, are willing to see their fellow town worthies so publicly disgraced. There is no other known explanation for the comparatively few prosecutions for this kind of assault on the environment.

It is not corruption. It is the blind eye turned by burgher against burgher who infringes the law, statutory or common, the wink which is as good as a nod, which passes for esprit de corps or town pride in Britain. It is the evil of local government, which puts power into local groups who are too often used to operating on a social rather than a public scale. It is based on

100

the principle of democracy, a principle which might well be adjudged to have failed at its local, social level. If local authorities cannot control the pollutant assault on our environment nobody can, and the record of local councils in this matter is one of untold failure.

This is not the place to argue local government reform generally, nor is there space to advocate the use of more executive and less elective authority in our shire and town halls. But if we examine pollution on a financial and control basis alone, we must accept that local authorities are underpowered in authority, and for social or lethargic reasons do not use the powers they have, and because they are dependent on central government for so much of their monies they cannot exercise them even if they wanted to.

If councillors are elected, and aldermen appointed, at a rate of one to every 5,000 of the population, and cannot, in groups of sixty, irrespective of their party, control the environment for which they are responsible, there must be a case for finding a group of people and a system which can. In this context, the idea of a single chairman or mayor, with three, five or seven elected assistants, and a similar number of very senior executive officers, is worthy of further consideration. Of course it will be argued that such an organisation cannot possibly deal with the minutes now handled by the average local council. Smaller local bodies at parish level might well be able to deal with smaller parish problems, though, and leave the all important environmental issues to people not bogged down with lesser issues. Alternatively, county and bigger town councils might well set up environmental committees with a senior official to advise them on matters which are more important than some of the subjects covered by some of their existing committees.

To fail to tackle the problem at very local roots can only add to the social disorder which is inherent in that problem. We have already seen that our planners do not plan for a happier environmental future because they do not have their priorities right. We have already discussed the failure to control births by family planning, and by default overcrowd our hospitals with abortion cases rather than see non-preventable diseases and ailments treated. We have seen evidence of roads and railways put before decent housing. We have also looked at the fact that man must earn his living before he considers what he is doing in that livelihood which will harm or even kill him and his fellows.

That is the way to social disorder. Much of it must be stopped at local level.

We are already an urban society. Urbanisation demands higher densities of population, more competition in every field for homes, for school places, for jobs and for material wealth. In that competitiveness the ancient roots of civilisation are being destroyed, particularly the root of family life. In the battle for homes, families have been split and parental control has too often vanished, leaving youngsters to their own uncontrolled indulgences. It is they who are the key to much of the increase in crime, particularly violent crime, which is rising at a rate approaching 10 per cent more cases a year. It is they who are the victims of drug addiction which has risen six-fold between 1960 and 1970. Their parents, as an escape from increased competition, the stress and strains of modern urban life, have turned to drink. Where else do we find Britain's half a million alcoholics who have made their condition the second or third most serious disease in the country?

Look at those facts and figures once more. And in the social disorder to which those figures are pointing will be found yet another clue to the picture of Britain in the year 2000.

If we do not control urbanisation and the progress alleged to go with it, no one is going to hold down crime, drug addiction, alcoholism, nor will they be able to stop the degenerative diseases if they do not tackle pollution. Country folk, rather than town dwellers, by more natural living have a better health record. Not for them the polluted air which brings heart disease, bronchitis and lung cancer. Nor do they rely so much on the sophisticated carbohydrates which, together with tinned additives, help produce so many of the new diseases with which our National Health Service is plagued.

Mr Aneuran Bevan's 1948 estimate for a Service free for all would have cost the taxpayer £120,000,000 per year, reckoning without those 'new' ailments which forced a more recent Minister, Mr Richard Crossman, to multiply that figure seventeen times by 1970. If his figure of £2,000,000,000 could undo the harm of unnatural living it would be money well spent, but there is more to modern ill health and the cost of it than that. The modern man with his drugs is building up an immunity to existing drugs and will continue to seek more antidotes, so that the modern methods of treating ailments must create their own ailments and demand more drugs, and more money, to put those right and so on.

Ill health, directly attributable to modern living, robs the nation of valuable working hours. Idle offices and factory benches reduce the goods we manufacture and the services we provide in both quantity and quality. In turn, Britain, so dependent on export, must lose out. The cost of manufacturing products and providing services must, therefore, rise, and in doing so price us out of the markets we seek so desperately.

That, in short, is the way to economic crises, to inflation, to devaluation, and to a material pauperism which will not be solved by joining or living off our European cousins in the Common Market of Europe. Britain may yet choose to join Europe for mutual progress or survival, but there cannot be a common good in one nation, Britain or any other, being unable to meet its commitments and pay its way in such a union. Already the price is said to be too high. That price will be beyond Britain's means if the root causes are not dealt with with urgency and resoluteness.

Her Majesty's Government in *The Protection of the Environment: The Fight Against Pollution* put the issue thus:

'Economics. It is now widely realised that increase in material goods brings with it certain "diseconomies"' in terms of health, amenity, and the attractiveness of the environment. Sometimes these diseconomies can be measured in monetary terms; and many cost-benefit studies attempt to do this. But sometimes the damage is indirect and intangible, and cannot be brought into relationship with the measuring rod of money. Society must then make a value judgement on how much it is prepared to spend, it must then select the most economic method of achieving the desired result; and it must take account of the way in which different methods allocate the burden to different groups in society – consumers of the products concerned, or producers, or the taxpayer in general. There is no uniquely right answer to any of these questions. Government and an informed public opinion must continuously search for the best answer in each particular case.'

It is quite right to warn of the cost problem, but surely control is essential, even if it means abandoning some of our traditional rights, privileges and freedoms. The alternative may be far more disastrous. In a word, sui-genicide. Just because suicide, taking one's life by one's own hand is no longer a stigma, and unsuccessful attempts no longer a matter for the courts and punishable, we are not logically entitled to see man jointly plan and execute his own end in the name of such freedoms.

the not-so-final solution

Not chaos-like together chush'd and bruis'd,
But, as the world, harmoniously confused;
Where order in variety we see,
And where, tho' all things differ, all agree.
. . . Pope, *Windsor Forest*. 1. 13.

AND THERE you have all the ingredients for social destruction, for the great Armageddon of man against nature. What then are the prospects of the horizon we have chosen, A.D. 2000?

Forecasting such a scene, like demography, cannot be an exact matter, but a general picture drawn from particular trends. We know that one of the great economists, the Rev. Thomas Robert Malthus, predicted that population trends showed an increase in geometric progression, e.g., by people constantly doubling their numbers, while food production could only increase at the most algebraically in consecutive units, adding in quantity by the same amount. His predictions were accepted until people realised that the population did not rise in a pattern of 2, 4, 6, 8, but at a slower rate, while food increased not in a 1, 2, 3, 4 pattern but in fact much faster than the population.

Here we have given not arithmetic figures for the sake of argument but merely as illustrations of trends, and drawn conclusions from those trends, conclusions which will hold only if checks and balances are not employed. There is an anti-ecological school of thought abroad which believes that since previous thirty-year predictions have proved false we should ignore the new ones and do nothing. Rather should we take heed of the warnings and ensure that they come to nought.

A businessman can only forecast profits or losses on the balance sheet he sees before him. The study of environment is man's own balance sheet. We can marvel at its assets, from his earliest cave drawings to the greatest art works in our great galleries, from the theories of Galileo to the achievements of Cape Kennedy and the observations of Jodrell Bank, from the aeroplane of the Wright Brothers to the latest spacecraft of the astronauts. Yet we must weep at the liabilities dating from the massacre of the innocents, the extermination of the dodo, to the genocide of Belsen and Buchenwald, to the razing of Monte Cassino, Coventry Cathedral, and the destruction of Nagasaki and Hiroshima. Surely the profits are to be found in preserving the heritage of twenty million centuries, with the endless process of evolution of man, his animals and plants, the continents and oceans, the mountains, rivers, plains and forests, and all the living things which have enjoyed them. What can be done about the losses? Of course some species have become extinct and have been replaced by other species, but man in his speed has stepped up the extinction rate by four times the normal evolutionary process.

He chops down the trees, drains the marshes, pollutes the rivers and seas, the atmosphere and soil, so that the relationship and reliance of his fellow men and other living things is broken. When man and animals cannot evolve a change as rapid as that of the habitat then they can only die, too.

It has become something trite rather than challenging to cry for preservation, conservation, anti-pollution, and the rest of the demands of ecological study, but there are reasons, compelling reasons why these appeals should be heeded. For man cannot live without belief, without beauty, without science, and without economic foundation. In between his bouts of destruction and creation, he employs a conscience, and that demands that he does not unnecessarily destroy other living things. His sense of pleasure, to behold things of beauty with the eye, prompts him to preserve and create things which are attractive and not ugly, so that when delights like the countryside have no material benefit to him, he wants them because they give him happiness.

Science must be harnessed to improve his lot, but his sense of conscience and beauty tells him that when this improvement harms other living things his employment of scientific knowledge has gone too far. Similarly, it is not only scientifically wrong to destroy wild life because it so often has an economic value to him in the production of food to eat, scenery to enjoy, and the provision of areas where he can enjoy his leisure time.

But man is a paradox and while he would admit these four reasons for preserving this planet, he often subconsciously and absent-mindedly behaves contrary to these precepts. Out of this emerges the picture of the year A.D. 2000. It is a picture of our planet, earth, without international control, and Britain, without national control or planning, developing contrary to man's knowledge and beliefs. It is a picture not necessarily built on logic, but built on probability, taking into account all the factors now known.

We have tended to isolate Britain in this picture merely because we are British, but all the factors known must include those factors from overseas. Thus, if we fear, as fear we must, an unchecked birth explosion in Britain, it is not because ours is the fastest growing birthrate. It is because we are inter-dependent on other countries which may well have bigger birth rate problems than we have. Consequently, if an underdeveloped country, by nature, or by economic gradual development has a fast rising birth rate and that country sells Britain food then it must affect us. Similarly, any evils which affect food production in such countries must also affect us.

The picture must, therefore, be one of gloom, for it would be naive to pretend or assume that the checks and balances, rules and regulations, laws and controls which have been ignored for centuries to protect us will suddenly be adopted and put into effect with such speed that they will save us from the destruction which is expected to overtake us within a mere thirty years. In those thirty years much can be done, but, alas, not that much. That is why we should look with seriousness rather than cynicism at the country we are creating, or failing to create, for ourselves.

We are, with thirty years to go, a somewhat smug people with almost enough to eat for all and and most of the able bodied among us with a reasonable expectancy of life, yet who are in fear, fear of losing our jobs at each economic crisis, but at the same time demanding more leisure time. We have not got enough field or facility for leisure nor an adequate method of transport from our homes to our places of work or play. Yet in case we do not live our lives to the full we increase the developments to the targets we fear the most.

Economically, we live in a free for all jungle in which the labour bargaining groups are like animals seeking the prize female in the pack. Sociologically, we grasp for anything and everything within or without reach, not heeding the needs let alone ambitions of our fellows. Politically, we vote across party lines for the most beneficial short-term benefits the election candidates can offer. Agriculturally, we believe in our daily bread but not so much in tomorrow's. In all, we represent man in his most simple, sinful form, and although we didn't invent them, we are guilty of all the seven capital errors of living, proud, wrathful, envious, lusty, gluttonous, avaricious and slothful. And we are perhaps not conscious of any of those dismal qualities.

When Mr Average Briton, that mythical figure of surveys, steps out into the twenty-first century, he is most likely to be a slum dweller, unless the traditionalists who destroyed the concept of High Paddington relent for his sake. That was the concept of building up and up – originally over Paddington, London, railway station – so that within one vertical complex a resident could find all his daily needs of home, rest, work, shops, churches, and leisure. Without that type of construction, he will have to attempt to share the limited acreage available to the expectant population.

Already, the Royal Institute of British Architects has prepared a near term blueprint for London.

This report on London 1981 has been proposed by Mr Charles McKean, secretary of the RIBA London Region which represents 3,300 architects and planners. Assisted by six members of the London Environment Group, he finds that the original brief

108

for the Greater London Development Plan was misconceived. The London Government Act states that the plan should 'lay down considerations of general policy with respect to the use of land in the various parts of Greater London, in particular guidance as to the future roads system'. The group points out that the second part of this brief is incompatible with the first. It calls for a roads plan which is not merely a matter of sub-strategy but deals with actual traffic tactics. The general transportation strategy is never really discussed. Thus the GLC is given the scope to produce neither a master plan in the best sense, nor a detailed structure plan. The result, says the report, is a plan which is 'hopelessly biased towards the roads programme to the extent of omitting all but the most scanty reference to the real problem of transportation'.

The report also criticises Professor Buchanan's Ringway Study, commissioned by the GLC to 'interpret the transportation strategy of the GDLP and demonstrate its feasibility'. Buchanan confuses 'transportation' with 'roads policy' since he fails to mention public transport. His statement that 'the motor vehicle is clearly the mainstay of transport in London' is unsupported, the report comments. The lack of discussion of the relative merits of different sections of the Ringways is 'a major omission'.

The report quotes Buchanan's argument that 'the development of a national system of inter-city motorways requires as a logical consequence a complementary provision of urban motorways. With this last argument,' the report says, 'any discussion of benefit to Londoners is dropped. The new roads are not to help Londoners, but to complete the national pattern of roads'.

The report comments scathingly: 'This is hardly a good justification of a road system which may cost almost as much as the rest of the national network which is already constructed.' And it is no less damning in its condemnation of the secondary roads system. 'It seems likely to have the most disastrous environmental consequences on London. It will destroy most of the historic areas of London, disrupt communities, and harm the environment since the roads which are to be widened for

109

increased traffic flow are those which historically are the community centres.'

The report urges that the whole concept should be rethought and replanned, basing the alignment of roads along the perimeters of community areas.

On the environmental factors of congestion, noise, vibration, air pollution and amenity the report says there are no specific proposals in the GLDP to deal with these problems.

'The GLC has no plan of action. Any conflict between pedestrian and traffic is to be resolved by putting the pedestrian either underground or over a bridge – whilst traffic continues uninterrupted and increased on the roads at ground level.'

The London Region will be presenting its evidence on the GLDP at various stages in the public inquiry. In order to monitor the inquiry from the start, the region is mounting what could be the most extensive operation in membership participation ever undertaken by a RIBA region.

It is calling on the 40,000 architects and architectural students in London to give up some time to attend the inquiry. Each person willing to take part on any given day will be asked to file a report on the proceedings.

The aim is not only to have continuous reportage by observers, but to encourage the participation of architects in the inquiry.

Instead, the RIBA group foresees the kind of London in which central London offices are adapted to provide housing accommodation. Aided by Government grants, the provision of flats would be financed by business concerns for their staff, the aim being to revitalise the central area and prevent a fall in population.

The cost of the road system would be helped by pricing the roads at 5s. per car mile travelled. Londoners should know how much any vehicle on a stretch of road really costs the community. They must decide whether this cost should be borne by all residents, or only by the drivers.

Better transport facilities could be ensured by the creation of transport interchanges at strategic perimeter points. Their free car parking facilities would reduce the number of commuters travelling into central London by car. The interchanges could be combined with freight depots.

Next would come the construction of orbital tube lines and the extension of existing lines. Underground lines are far cheaper to construct than motorways, can carry more people, and have less harmful environmental effects than roads.

The traditional idea of road and rail services alongside, or the discarded modern view of having them underneath high rise blocks, would vanish. The Group prefers alignment of motorways and major road schemes at roof-top level with houses built below them. 'The quietest place in the neighbourhood of a motorway is, in fact, underneath it,' says the group. As the land would in any case have to be bought, the provision of housing space beneath them would be cheaper than elsewhere.

Caesar's ban on day commercial traffic would be extended to the banning of heavy goods vehicles in London. There is no valid reason why all goods vehicles of any size should be permitted unlimited access throughout London. This is particularly relevant in view of the proposed heavy lorry size and loading increases.

At the same time, there must be a restriction of commuter cars in Inner London. Special parking permits could be issued to cut the number of people travelling to work by car. If there is less car parking provision, they will make the public switch to public transport.

This view is open to question unless there is a very severe restriction on street parking. Although there is no national private garage count, there is no doubt that the majority of car owners keep their vehicles on the public highway without paying for that privilege. If the Government is unwilling or unable to restrict the manufacture, sale or use of private cars, either by law or by swingeing taxation, then that switch to public transport will not take place. Nor will it come about by the RIBA group's limited view that clearways and lanes should be established for buses only, and that no secondary roads should be improved without the provision of bus lanes. This would provide equality of transport facility for public transport passengers and car drivers.

111

The Group is quite rightly sociologically minded in dealing with pedestrian traffic. Pedestrianisation of particularly well used shopping precincts like Bond Street and Kings Cross is a worthy notion, but the question of goods access is bound to arise, even if delivery is possible at only out-of-shopping-hours. The Group also points out that the usual futuristic idea of walkways at an upper level would bring the risk of encouraging crime and attacks on pedestrians.

The architects and planners do not ignore the need for greater emphasis on conservation, which they define as the best use of existing materials.

Obviously, even the most wide-sweeping plans for construction or redevelopment must not raze the unarguable amenities which should be preserved. This is a matter of judgement; which must be exercised well for the Group pinpoints the signal error of much city planning. Instead of talking, discussing and thinking about making a city a better place in which to live and work, those responsible tend to think only of planning an economic unit. And open spaces, scenery of beauty, works of art, historic buildings and the like are seldom economical to maintain. They must be maintained unless we are to live in a cultural desert, and rather than say 'this must go because it is uneconomical' it would be preferable to find out 'how can we make it economical'.

Mr Average Briton will doubtlessly survive all that, the short-term, and part of the economic v. uneconomic battle, but in the year 2000 he is much more likely to find himself as an urban dweller in a high rise environment, and the dwindling members of what was once known as rural England will be, in the majority, the middle aged retired, the leisure seekers, and those, such as scientists, whose work is best carried out well away from large townships. This will come about because by then the planners will have been forced to accept that there is only one way to build in these tiny islands and that is upwards. While today we speak about decentralisation, pleading with office organisations and industries to move away from our city centres, tomorrow will find those new decentralised centres already new cities.

Mr A. B. may well arise, in his multi-storied apartment block, with all the push-button automation of future living, but it should be his social relationships which will concern us. His medicine cabinet will be jam packed with every sort of birth control device, intended for both the male and the female. For he will know only too well the financial and imprisonment penalties to be meted out to those who overbreed. As a constant reminder there will be hanging on the wall a framed certificate from the local population planning and control board giving him permission to have one child, certifying that he and his partner are in sound health, both in mind and body, and can make material provision for that one child. There will still be a repugnance to the idea of a master race, in which only those of Anglo Saxon stock, or proven IQ, or proven financial means should breed, but the pressures of the old century, and the challenges of the new, will have already forced these limitations on the nation.

The responsibility for not breeding, since man and woman will be equal under all laws, will be a joint one. To practice birth control will be mandatory on every person after puberty, and there will be financial penalties for those responsible for a woman conceiving, in astronomical fees for abortion, in punitive fines for rape, and worse for those who conceal the existence of an unauthorised child. For how else will the State to come be able to control the birth explosion, care for the living, and plan for the future?

Medical science may not have eradicated all disease. History suggests that each century has its own specialities in causes for natural fatality, such as fevers, tuberculosis, and cancer. The emphasis is more likely to be on research and prevention, and, inevitably, psychiatry for modern living will take on a new ascendency. Our male and female will find within their own apartment block the clinic, doctor's surgery, and short stay mini-hospital. They will leave their only child in a creche there, and after a breakfast of concentrated foods, leave for work.

That food, owing to global natural and man-made shortages, may well have reached the pill, tablet and capsule stage. And while such foodstuffs will have replaced the tastes of today –

113

even more so than today's tastes have replaced those of thirty years ago – they will be highly chemical. At the same time they will be designed to prevent some of today's excesses which cause obesity and attendant evils. Eating at home will be simple, and if eating out is more elaborate, it will not take place in establishments designed only for eating. The outing will be taken up by entertainment while eating, and, if educationalists succeed, by using the occasion for mass lectures and teach-ins at the same time. For there will be hardly a better opportunity to find a captive audience to receive further education, particularly on the increasing problems of future living. Since food is reduced to swallowing pills, and the art of conversation has already largely vanished, the idea of eating out will be transformed into a public good.

After the first meal of the day, the couple will deposit their child in the creche, and ride in the lift to the roof to take the only means of transport available, public transport by fast motorway, rail, mono-rail, helicopter or vertical take-off aircraft. The centuries-old domination of the land by road and rail routes will have at least started to disappear, and the use of overhead routes, by relying on transport-on-stilts, will be the only way to free the land below for some form of conservation, either for greenery or for remaining agricultural use. Similarly, the building of out of town airports for all flying, and the consequent difficult journeys to town centres, will have been considerably modified. Those airports will be limited to trans-globe flying, while shorter stop air routes will depend on vertical take-off transport which can fly from roof to roof, from city to city.

If private transport is permitted at all, it will be extremely restricted and its operation rigidly enforced. Mr A. B., if he can prove a public and/or business need for a private car, well over and above his social need, he will be permitted one vehicle only. And this car will be permitted for use only certain roads, maybe at certain times, when commercial transport is either totally barred or similarly limited to certain hours. It will be further subject to fixed parking spaces wherever it goes, and these will be mostly inside, not outside, living and business or industrial premises. It will also be so subject to mechanical and driving fitness tests, that possession or use of such a method of transport will be regarded as a highly privileged asset. Penalties for faulty mechanism, bad driving, or anti-social use will be necessarily swingeing.

Mr A. B. will be essentially a member of the collar-and-tie labour force, for the extension of that group will inevitably continue. The 1970 working population of some 25,000,000 people – 16,000,000 male and 9,000,000 female – shows a steady fall in manual occupations and a greater growth in desk jobs. There are exceptions, but broadly speaking the productive and manufacturing industries show falls, while the professional and administrative groups show rises. Down are agriculture and mining, for reasons already explained, as are transport, probably because of industrial uncertainty, textiles and clothing. But rises have been shown in food, chemical and automative businesses. All told, the tendency is towards the pushing of pens, the lighting of bunsen burners and the programming of computers and away from the hewing of wood and drawing of water.

Running down of basic industries will throw more and more on to the labour market, which is already at capacity and will be overburdened by each school-leaving army. The only answer, and one certainly reached by Mr A. B.'s time, will be the further rising of the school-leaving age, and the dropping of the retirement age, so that the working population will be more, but not more fully, occupied, working shorter hours and a shorter week. The four-day week still being argued in 1970 will more certainly be a natural, unarguable three-day week by the end of the century. And the question will not be how much more work can a man do, but how much more leisure should occupy his time. How much more leisure activities will have to be provided when the weekend becomes longer than the week will be one of the problems of the time.

Our model man is more likely to travel to work on a shorter national or regional shift basis. All the pleadings for people to stagger their working hours, to help an already overburdened public transport system, have failed. This failure of appeal and of the system, plus an ever increasing working population, will demand that working hours are compulsorily fixed. More than that, so will the starting and finishing times.

Before Mr A. B. is at work at 10.30 a.m. or 11 a.m. or later, the commercial deliveries on short runs will have been completed leaving the roads free for him, if he uses a private car, to travel to his business. This travelling distance will be necessarily limited, and he will be under penalty to return to his own locality by a certain hour, so that the later daily commercial deliveries can continue to be run. Without such restrictions, even the largest imaginable network of motorways will be over-crowded, and the resulting traffic jamming of out-of-city inter-sections chaotic. So out of this chaos will come the order of the roads, better hourly use, better density, and better timing.

Work for our man is more likely to be a communal affair. This will be a natural necessity for a number of reasons. First the fall of the one-man and small business will be complete, and virtually all commercial and industrial organisations will be of substantial size. Secondly, the much vaunted managerial revolution, followed by the executive ambition, will have become such a competitive field that the status of title holders will become meaningless. (As W. S. Gilbert wrote: 'When everybody's somebody, then nobody's anybody.') In this state of equality in a large organisation, Mr A. B. will go to work in a large open planned office or laboratory, in which the multitudinous small, one-man, or one-man-and-a-secretary offices are obsolete. In this atmosphere he will be able to mix more freely, more socially than hitherto.

This is not to say that class barriers, with us since the beginning of time, will vanish, but the distinctions will be between different industries rather than between people in the same industry. More people will commute, under our orderly time table, and nearly all will wear suits, not overalls. They are likely to find that social intercourse at work, even though the working hours are much shorter, will be far more extensive than will be possible in their home communities. At work facilities for this social exchange will be more easily arranged than in the monolithic homes, autoshops, creches and clinics buildings in which they live. At home, the population and demand for private

116

living space, will put social clubs and the like at a premium. So what is to be done about leisure time?

Television, then colour television, and then the small receiver inserted in the skull by simple surgery, will be the marks of progress in the sound and vision, learning and entertainment field. All of which reduces further actual social gatherings. The use of satellites to transmit more and more global programmes will keep the average man from his fellows. And it may be that only by returning to simple endeavours, such as sport and adventure (mostly of a foolhardy nature such as aerobatics, motor racing, parachuting and the like), will the social-cum-leisure problem be solved. The idea of an extension of spectator sports to four days a week, without a similar expansion of participatory and competitive games, is a possibility which will have to be curbed.

Imagine Mr A. B. working a four, five or six-hour day for three days a week and spending the remaining four days watching football, Britain's only successful spectator recreation. Boredom will compel him to seek other leisure pursuits. It is essential, as time catches up with the environmental crisis, that further education – particularly in ecology – will be necessary, and even compulsory. He may well be required to attend further schooling, as will his wife. The schools may well bring back the carrot-and-stick philosophy of olden times, but instead of rewarding the hardworking, and beating and depriving the slothful, greater social rewards, in finance, housing, and social privilege, including car travel and permission to breed another child, might go to the citizen who contributes more to society by adult studies. And the greater contribution he makes in practical terms, so much greater should be the rewards.

Socialists might be horrified at the thought, but so will Conservatives, for neither traditional political belief will have any place in the end of the century pattern. The idea of giving from each according to his ability to each according to his needs will have long since vanished. The able, as distinct from the hereditarily weathly – a long since dead group of people – will have increasingly dictated the pace and pattern of life. Theoretically, there should be no needy, but they will be increasingly classed as unable. They will not have kept up with the able and they may well become a submerged minority. They will be encouraged to become able, but the State, as it moves into the twenty-first century, will have called a halt to the handouts to those who will not help themselves.

Mr A. B.'s hypothetical father was in one of the vanishing industries. Was it mining or agriculture? No matter, he could foresee the disappearance of his livelihood many years before and decided to get out while there was time, and re-train for another industry. Unfortunately, many of his fellow workers saw the same prospect but refused to change their occupations, preferring to rely on the State-ordained redundancy payments that would come when their farm or mine closed down. They did not foresee that those payments, more generous though they had become, would not last forever, nor would they be sufficient to help them also re-train for other work. As a result, they found themselves at fairly advanced years, but nowhere near retirement age, without money and without work. For them the twenty-first century would become a curse. Their belief in State benefits, supplementary benefits, subsidies, and other manna from the mint, had been encouraged by national and local government, by employers and by trade unions. But long before the 2000th year, the nation had found that the majority was in danger of, or actually in the process of, living off the minority and a halt had to be called.

Since dependence by one section of the community on another will become intolerable, inter-dependence will have to replace it, and thus those who do not contribute must consequently suffer.

Both Mr A. B. senior and his son, during those courses, will find that the fragmentation of unions, with their chalk mark disputes, over who should do what, which has already reached the ridiculous, will end, and just as businesses merge into larger units, so will the unions. The unions, in an age of more skilled people, will tend to be attached to trades as they were originally intended, rather than to a level of skills. If the automative and chemical industries emerge, as expected, as the most powerful in the land, then their workers will be represented by their own industries rather than large omnibus organisations which try to represent people of all trades in different industries. And this tendency should mark a welcome end to cross-union poaching and demarcation disputes.

If this pattern of life does not suit socialists and trade unionists, it will bring no more happiness to Conservatives. The sun having long since set on the empire, the removal of competition as a be-all and end-all of private enterprise, and the devotion of more profits to future endeavour will cause a considerable rethink among the political right wing. Social responsibility is more likely to be the watchword than individual liberty. For the abuse of freedoms which has already led to over population, to air and sea pollution, to the ruination of the earth and its scenery, can only be replaced by curbs, preferably designed to ensure freedom at the price of responsibility. And it is unlikely that such a state can be reached without better designed and more simple laws, but hopefuly without more governmental control. Only a lawyer would deny that the law can be made more simple, but in reforming the statute book, an admittedly slow process, there are many who believe this can be done.

The move to codify the law, to lay down degrees of theft, fraud and murder is already growing in 1970. It is to be hoped that this process will eventually lead to a basis of laws built on the ancient premise: do unto others as you would be done by. This is an over-simplification, but too much of lawyers' and courts' time is taken up by cases of individual versus individual. Rather that the concentration should be on the individual versus society and vice versa.

Criminal statistics suggest that crime, as we know it today, will continue to increase, and, because of lack of outlets for youth, except at political demonstrations which they do not understand, and sports events which they do not appreciate, there will be more violence. All this will lead to more and more people occupying prisons, and remaining idle. This is an already evident truth, and the only suggestion which has emerged is that probation officers and workers should deal more with those people who are now sent to prison, the evidence being that where there are more probation workers the jail population is correspondingly less.

Under a system which puts society before the individual, prison could be reserved for only the most serious of crimes, while repayment and reparation for robbery and damage could be enforced so rigidly that such wrongdoings would not pay. At present prison restrictions tend to be largely ameliorated by comforts that were never intended, thus making incarceration bearable if not pleasant. Better that the wrongdoer makes amends before being regarded as free from his sins. After all, there can hardly be more waste of manpower than driving people to prison, and there can hardly be less satisfaction in the system which leaves a man without his money, or without his physical health, while his robber or assailant is sent to prison without further practical amends.

This then is the society Mr A. B. should see. The reader is not bound to accept it. The author takes responsibility for the forecast. Only the evidence can be relied upon to point to the year 2000. Only those who read this book will be able to halt the trends, divert the energies, preserve the best of our heritage, and ensure that the worst traits of our natural behaviour are curbed. Only he who sees the threat of too many people in too confined space, of garbage where living things should be, of smoke-filled air where the sky should be clear, of dirty rivers which should run clear and free, can decide what sort of place Britain will be.

The picture is not as gloomy as some have painted it. Only if things go on as they are – to use a politician's safeguarding phrase – will Mr A. B. face a life of restriction from the cradle to the grave. At best, he cannot hope to have the freedom – to abuse, to pollute, to destroy – that he has today. At worst, he will be a victim of his own destruction. It is possible that by choosing today, man may be able to ensure that a bearable if not happy medium may be arrived at so that his successors inherit only some of the evils, but receive some of the benefits of his work. It is, alas, a possibility rather than a probability, for destruction has reached more than the proportions of a tide, and man, in the role of King Canute, cannot conceivably stop the tide. It is simple to say that trends of thirty years ago have been stopped as were trends thirty years before that. But it is more true to say that those tendencies were halted or diverted by spontaneous piecemeal measures or fashion changing attitudes. How much better to ensure that inclinations which are doubtful or wrong should be deliberately thwarted than left to chance or last-minute decisions.

Whatever Mr A. B. may earn or enjoy, it will be useless to him if his parents have not realised that there is a limit beyond which the population should not go. They must realise that his future is now being decided by them. If they, by their air and water pollution, and by irresponsible experiments, change the world's heat balance, they may well decide his weather for him, and decide whether he will freeze, or drown. Their raids on the bowels of the earth, shortening the supplies of metals, like gold, lead and zinc, may deprive him of their benefits, or at least by hoisting the prices, put them out of his reach.

They and their forebears have been cavalier in their relations with nature, and this is the first time in history that they have the opportunity of pausing, consciously and systematically to take comprehensive stock of their surroundings. In taking stock they may well arrest the depredations inflicted so carelessly on the natural system, which heaven knows exists in an intricate balance. If they do not think of themselves, and of Mr A. B. of the year 2000, then ecological disaster is assured. If they do, there is hope.

Of course, no politician, no scientist, no writer can predict the future on trends alone. There are large gaps in the experts' environmental knowledge, but at least much of what is wrong can easily be identified. That is why it is necessary to think of Mr A. B. senior's environment today, not to master nature, but to master Mr A. B. and his fellows, his institutions and his technology. In this way the doom so easily predicted can so easily be avoided. It will need drastic changes. It will need enormous sums of money.

People may ultimately have to forego some of the conveniences of twentieth century living and pay higher prices for goods and services, but the price cannot be too high. For some of that price is already being misspent. If the Government wishes to give grants for public works, directly or indirectly, for water and sewer development, let them give it to control development rather than to use it for uncontrolled expanding development. If it is for housing and new town development, let it be for those areas where the awareness of urban and rural blight is greatest. And if those who receive grants continue in ignorance of the future they are building let the grants be withheld.

Otherwise Mr A. B. will be a victim of the social disorder here described. If Britain falls in its competitiveness, there can only be unemployment. Unemployment will again produce crime because starving people must eat. Out of that unrest the extremist political movements will incite riots. Riots may mean bloodshed and death. The choice of living or dying for a better year A.D. 2000 is in the hands of the people.

Acknowledgements and Bibliography

WHEN *The Sun* newspaper passed to new proprietorship in the autumn of 1969, the new Editor, Mr Larry Lamb, appointed me his News Editor and instructed me that the newspaper would tell the people in stark, simple terms, in news, in features and in pictures the environmental crises they are facing. It was from the collection of this material for *The Sun* that the contents of this book emerged. I am grateful, therefore, to Mr Lamb for his encouragement in the production of this work, and to the following societies, organisations, and publications, for information, for guidance and for the example they have set:

Central Scientific Unit on Environmental Pollution, Stories Gate, London, S.W.1.

Ministry of Technology (Oil and Air Pollution), Gunnels Wood Road, Stevenage, Herts.

Inter-Governmental Maritime Consultative Organisation, (I.M.C.O.), 22 Berners Street, London, W.1.

Nature Conservancy, 19 Belgrave Square, London, S.W.1.

World Wildlife Fund, 7–8 Plumtree Court, London, E.C.4.

Council for Nature, Zoological Gardens, Regents Park, London, N.W.1.

Noise Abatement Society, 6 Old Bond Street, London, W.1.

Society for the Promotion of Nature Reserves, The Manor House, Alford, Lincs.

The National Trust, 42 Queen Anne's Gate, London, S.W.1.

Society for the Protection of Ancient Buildings, 55 Great Ormond Street, W.C.1.

Royal Society for the Protection of Birds, The Lodge, Sandy, Beds.

Botanical Society of the British Isles, c/o Department of Botany, British Museum (Natural History), Cromwell Road, London, S.W.7.

Council for the Preservation of Rural England, 4 Hobart Place, London, S.W.1.

Council for Small Industries in Rural Areas, Advisory Service Division, 35 Camp Road, London, S.W.19.

Countryside Commission, 1 Cambridge Gate, London, N.W.1.

Civic Trust, 18 Carlton House Terrace, London, S.W.1.

Ramblers Association, 124 Finchley Road, London, N.W.3.

The journals of many of those organisations have provided much food for thought, as has the very newly published *Ecologist* monthly magazine, and particularly *Wildlife,* the quarterly publication of the World Wildlife Fund. Where such journals have been directly quoted acknowledgements have been given on the page. Even with so many sources and their publications, the views expressed in this book are entirely mine.

After the writing of this book was completed two notable publications were announced which should be included in this short bibliography. They are:

The Doomsday Book, Gordon Rattray Taylor (Thames and Hudson);

The Ebony Ark: Black Africa's battle to save its wild life, Eric Robins (Barrie and Jenkins).

Earlier works which may be taken as a guide rather than a detailed list of sources for students, are:

Too Many: A study of earth's biological limitations, G. Borgstrom (Macmillan, 1969).

Extinct and Vanishing Animals, V. Ziswiler (Longmans, 1968).

Vanishing Animals of the World, R. Fitter (Kaye and Ward, 1968).

The Torrey Canyon, J. E. Smith, editor (Cambridge University Press, 1968).

Impingement of Man on the Oceans, D. Hood, editor (Wiley, 1970).

The Soil and its Fertility, H. Teuscher (Chapman and Hall, 1960).

Land, Water and Food, H. Addison (Chapman and Hall, 1961).

The New Scientist, weekly, London.

The New Society, weekly, London.

Nature, weekly, London.

Your Environment, quarterly, London.

The Population Bomb, P. Ehrlich (Ballantine, New York, 1968).

Silent Spring, R. Carson (Crest, N.Y., 1969).

Man's Role in Changing the Face of the Earth, W. Thomas (University of Chicago Press, 1956).

This is the American Earth, Ansel Adams, Nancy Newhall (Sierra Club, U.S., 1968 – photo book).

NEL BESTSELLERS

Science Fiction

F.2658	GLORY ROAD	*Robert Heinlein* 7/6
F.2844	STRANGER IN A STRANGE LAND	*Robert Heinlein* 12/-
F.2630	THE MAN WHO SOLD THE MOON	*Robert Heinlein* 6/-
F.2386	PODKAYNE OF MARS	*Robert Heinlein* 6/-
F.2449	THE MOON IS A HARSH MISTRESS	*Robert Heinlein* 8/-
F.2754	DUNE	*Frank Herbert* 12/-

War

F.2695	THE MAN THEY COULDN'T KILL	*Dennis Holman* 5/-
F.2484	THE FLEET THAT HAD TO DIE	*Richard Hough* 5/-
F.2805	HUNTING OF FORCE Z	*Richard Hough* 5/-
F.2494	P.Q.17—CONVOY TO HELL	*Lund Ludlam* 5/-
F.2423	STRIKE FROM THE SKY—THE BATTLE OF BRITAIN STORY	
		Alexander McKee 6/-
F.2471	THE STEEL COCOON	*Bentz Plagemann* 5/-
F.2645	THE LONGEST DAY	*Cornelius Ryan* 5/-
F.2146	THE LAST BATTLE (illustrated)	*Cornelius Ryan* 12/6

Western

Walt Slade—Bestsellers

F.2506	LEAD AND FLAME	*Bradford Scott* 4/-
F.2634	THE SKY RIDERS	*Bradford Scott* 4/-
F.2648	OUTLAW ROUNDUP	*Bradford Scott* 4/-
F.2649	RED ROAD TO VENGEANCE	*Bradford Scott* 4/-
F.2669	BOOM TOWN	*Bradford Scott* 4/-
F.2687	THE RIVER RAIDERS	*Bradford Scott* 4/-

General

F.2721	EROTIC EDWARDIAN FAIRY TALES	*Anon.* 6/-
F.2420	THE SECOND SEX	*Simone De Beauvoir* 8/6
F.2234	SEX MANNERS FOR MEN	*Robert Chartham* 5/-
F.2531	SEX MANNERS FOR ADVANCED LOVERS	*Robert Chartham* 5/-
F.2766	SEX MANNERS FOR THE YOUNG GENERATION	*Robert Chartham* 5/-
F.2374	SEX WITHOUT GUILT	*Albert Ellis Ph.D.* 8/6
U.2366	AN ABZ OF LOVE	*Inge and Sten Hegeler* 10/6
U.2851	A HAPPIER SEX LIFE (illustrated)	*Dr. Sha Kokken* 12/-
F.2136	WOMEN	*John Philip Lundin* 5/-
F.2333	MISTRESSES	*John Philip Lundin* 5/-
F.2511	SEXUALIS '95	*Jacques Sternberg* 5/-
F.2720	THE FIRST TIME	*Paul Tabori* 6/-
F.2584	SEX MANNERS FOR SINGLE GIRLS	*Dr. G. Valensin* 5/-
F.2592	THE FRENCH ART OF SEX MANNERS	*Dr. G. Valensin* 5/-

Mad

S.3702	A MAD LOOK AT OLD MOVIES	5/-
S.3523	BOILING MAD	5/-
S.3496	THE MAD ADVENTURES OF CAPTAIN KLUTZ	5/-
S.3719	THE QUESTIONABLE MAD	5/-
S.3714	FIGHTING MAD	5/-
S.3613	HOWLING MAD	5/-
S.3477	INDIGESTIBLE MAD	5/-

NEL P.O. BOX 11, FALMOUTH, CORNWALL

Please send cheque or postal order. Allow 9d. per book to cover postage and packing (Overseas 1/- per book).

Name...

Address ....

....

Title ....
(AUGUST)